THE ILLUMINATION CODEX
GATEWAY TWO PART THREE

New Earth Transmissions

Future Timelines of Gaia

MICHAEL GARBER

MICHAEL GARBER

Printed in the United States of America
First Printing 2021
First Edition 2021

Second Edition

ISBNs:
Softcover 978-1-959561-09-5
eBook 978-1-959561-10-1

10 9 8 7 6 5 4 3 2 1

THE
ILLUMINATION
CODEX

Table of Contents

ACKNOWLEDGMENTS

I bow in humble recognition of the One Light of Consciousness, the Source of my being and the source of all knowledge and wisdom. I give gratitude to the Supreme for dreaming me into existence and allowing me to have the conscious experience of life and the crafting of this codex.

I bow in love and gratitude to my dear beloved partner Ron Amit, a true gift of the Divine, for all the many ways he supports me in my life. I am blessed beyond measure to have such a brilliant master of love, compassion, and divine service to walk this earthly life with. Thank you for all that you do, seen and unseen, to amplify joy and higher consciousness for me and all beings in the Cosmos. I love you across all space, time, and dimensions.

I send gratitude to my friends and clients who have brought forth the lost stories of Creation through their Illuminated Quantum Healing hypnosis sessions. Thank you for being the powerful Light beacons that you are!

I send deep gratitude to my many modern scribes who assisted me in the transcription work. Thank you for helping me capture these incredible client stories so that the world can remember our cosmic divine heritage.

Bless all the beings, seen and unseen, who have helped me craft this material so that you, the reader, can be nourished on your path of Ascension. May you, the reader, be blessed infinitely and discover the highest truth of your being. May ascended consciousness, liberation, and divine unification be yours in this very life!

DEDICATION AND INVOCATION

This book is dedicated to the infinite expressions of our Oneself, for the celebration of our many incarnations, past, present, and future, and the lessons we have learned throughout eternity. May these words and the energy they carry be a potent force for awakening for all seekers of Unconditional Love and divine Truth. May this transmission support the reactivation and restoration of humanity's divine blueprint upon planet Earth and accelerate the realization of our eternal unity and oneness with all of Creation.

Let us join in prayer, honoring and sending gratitude to the Supreme Intelligent Source of Creation, the omniscient, omnipotent, omnipresent, transcendental Divine Source that is our True Nature.

Let us honor and send gratitude to the higher Light realms and the beings of Light who guide and protect Creation's evolution. Let us honor and send gratitude to our star lineages and those who support us from beyond the Earth. Let us receive your love and blessings now as we remember our cosmic ancestry and our role in the higher evolutionary plan for Creation.

Let us honor and send gratitude to our Earth Mother and her many dimensions and manifestations of Life including the animal, plant, bacterial, fungal, protozoan, mineral, crystalline, and elemental beings who contribute to her dynamic, regenerative biomes. These writings are offered as salve and balm to heal and bless our beloved Gaia, our Earth Mother and Divine Sister. May her waters be pure, her soil rich, her air clean, and may all beings, seen and unseen, within her living biofield know lasting peace forever and ever.

Let us honor and send gratitude to the wisdom and guidance from the seven directions of East, South, West, North, Above, Below, and Within. Let us call back our soul fragments scattered through time and space so that we may anchor ourselves HERE and NOW in this eternal moment of infinite potential to witness the unfolding manifestation of the Divine Plan.

Let us honor and send gratitude to the elements of Earth, Air, Fire, Water, and Ether that create the foundation of our evolutionary experience in form. May the Light of Consciousness awaken swiftly in each of us as we remember our True Nature beyond names and forms.

Let us honor and send gratitude to our ancestors and the many souls who have shared their light upon the Earth. Let us send special thanks to those who dedicated their lives to passing on the Mysteries and sacred knowledge of the Divine so that we may NOW stand at this Grand Turning of the Ages, with the support of all who have come and all who are destined to live upon this great Earth.

I call forth the full remembering of our divinity and the weaving of a new story of harmony and peace for all of Life upon the Earth. May we shed our stories of limitation and suffering and step forward into a new era as People of Light, cosmic co-citizens, and ambassadors for the Living Light of Creation.

Hallelujah! Jai! Aho! Blessed Be! Amen! And so, it is! Om!

GUIDANCE FOR READING THIS BOOK

The Illumination Codex is a multidimensional library for the path of Ascension. It is holographic by nature as each chapter contains a multitude of keycodes to activate ancient cellular memory and trigger multidimensional awareness and higher consciousness integration. As you read the material, your Inner Being will offer flashes of insight and higher perception into your awareness to assist you in healing, spiritual activation, and cosmic remembrance. I recommend using a highlighter, journaling your process, and using other resources to research and enhance your understanding of the topics presented in this book.

A major influence for this material comes from my work as a past-life regression hypnotherapist using the methods we have codified into a technique called Illuminated Quantum Healing (IQH). While in a deep hypnotic trance, my clients experience other lifetimes and other planetary civilizations and communicate with advanced intelligent species from beyond the Earth and Earth plane. The information contained in this book is a summary of my understanding of all that I have learned through my clients as they journeyed to the ancient past, probable timelines of the future, and higher planes of Light. There are many transcriptions of IQH sessions included in the book for you to have your own unique interpretation and multidimensional experience with the material.

This book contains a diverse collection of spiritual information from a variety of wisdom traditions that I have studied in my life. These writings are my own interpretations and understandings of these different concepts that have helped me in my awakening journey and do not necessarily speak for the lineages themselves. This presentation of information is meant as a collection of keys to unlock the wisdom that is already encoded within you. None of it is meant to become dogmatic as consciousness revelation and ascendency will open us continuously to higher and higher truths and understanding.

I confess that I share this transmission as a fellow traveler on the path of awakening. I have my own limitations, my own egoic nature, and my own struggles. I am capable of error and ignorance just as any other person. This presentation of information is what I have found along my path which has triggered awakening and helped me on my path back home to my Self. My prayer is that this book will become deeply meaningful for you and be a guiding light back to your own liberated being.

While reading this material, you may come across something in the text that triggers something within you that is uncomfortable. Maybe it is words that I use, perspectives that I share, or something else that may bring up resistance, judgment, anger, guilt, and so on. This is a wonderful opportunity to investigate the origin of the reactive mental and emotional patterns that create such experiences. The origin may come from earlier stages of your life or previous lifetimes. Use this as an opportunity to reconcile those parts of your consciousness through spiritual inquiry and self-study so that you may realize deeper states of wholeness and clarity.

This text is intended to activate 'gnosis,' a direct experience and knowledge of the divine presence within and around you. I do not recommend blind faith in any concept or religious doctrine. The information in this book is not meant to be treated as religious dogma that cannot be questioned or developed further. It is meant to be utilized to unlock the truth that lives within your very being. I am not writing this intending to change people's beliefs or convert anyone. I am simply relaying the summary of my life's research on the quest for spiritual truth. If something from the material does not resonate as truth in your heart, release it and move on to the next part of the transmission. Use the philosophy and information in this text to stimulate your expansion and the embodiment of YOUR deepest truth and to strengthen your relationship and innate connection with the Divine.

Another thing to mention is capitalization. You will notice that there are words that are not normally capitalized in other books and sacred texts that are capitalized in this text. My intention behind this was to add spiritual dimensionality to words that describe qualities or names of the Divine.

Typically, when I speak of light in this book, I am speaking about higher-dimensional, intelligently-encoded subtle energy and not conventional light from a light bulb. When I speak about "energy," I am speaking about subtle energy which exists beyond the visible light spectrum for most people. Many are becoming sensitive to subtle energy (i.e., multisensory, intuitive, psychic) and are developing the ability to sense and perceive this energy through extrasensory perception. All of humanity is evolving towards being able to perceive and interact with subtle energy and higher cosmic intelligence and consciousness.

The use of the term consciousness fluctuates throughout the book and can mean different things. When I speak of pure Consciousness I am speaking about your True Self as Source Consciousness, the Absolute, the Eternal Witness of all Creation, pure Awareness and Existence itself. Other times I will speak of consciousness as in variations of the mind such as unity consciousness or separation consciousness. All forms of consciousness, all experiences of the mind, borrow existence from the One Light of Consciousness and you are that!

I tried my best to organize this text in a way that can be read from front to back like any regular book, but it can also be read any way you feel intuitively called to read it. Part of the reason for the size of this codex is because it is difficult to explain one part without understanding many other components. In my effort to answer all potential and probable questions about ascension, I wrote everything I could on this multifaceted, multidimensional topic.

As you make your journey through this material, there are three stages to help integrate the information and use it to fuel your awakening to your True Nature:

Stage One: Listening (*Sravana*) As you read or listen to the material in this book, allow it to penetrate deeply and work with your inner philosophical understanding. Listen deeply to your Inner Being for there will be flashes of insight and knowing that emerge within your inner consciousness space.

Stage Two: Reflection (*Manana*) Try your best to understand the information contained in this book through self-inquiry and inner philosophical pondering. I am not asking for you to blindly believe any of this transmission. Think of this information as an active hypothesis. You do not have to believe it, but you can reflect over the information and see how it applies to your life.

Stage Three: Integration/Meditation (*Nididhyasana*) As you take in the words in stage one and convert the words to knowledge and understanding in stage two, you move into conviction and integration of knowledge in stage three as you crystallize and embody the Self-knowledge of "I am Pure Consciousness." As you go about your daily life, use the knowledge you have gained to interrupt habit and conditioned thought and re-direct your mind toward the Light of Consciousness that you are.

Gateways of Entry

Besides reading front-to-back or intuitively hopping around, I have created six gateways for you to enter the presentation of the material. I have created one large book that has all of the Illumination Codex material and separated the material into separately published volumes to make the information more digestible. The Gateways are as follows:

GATEWAY ONE: ASCENSION INITIATION: KEYS FOR HIGHER EVOLUTION gives an overall understanding of Ascension, reincarnation, universal law, and a theoretical and philosophical framework concerning Cosmic Evolution. This is an excellent place to start if you are open and eager to learn about these subjects and awakening, you may want to start in Gateway Three.

GATEWAY TWO: AKASHIC DATABASE contains a wide variety of Illuminated Quantum Healing session transcriptions describing key figures and events in the history of Creation, galactic history, ancient planetary history, and probable future timelines of New Earth from clients in hypnotic visionary states. This is a suitable place to enter the material if you already have a general understanding of multidimensionality, galactic civilizations, and the process of personal and planetary ascension. This gateway is conveniently separated into QUANTUM ORIGINS, COSMIC CHRIST TRANSMISSIONS, and NEW EARTH TRANSMISSIONS. If you find yourself resistant to those ideas and are new to these subjects. I recommend developing a meditation practice parallel to reading this material as the transcripts are deeply activating on multiple levels.

GATEWAY THREE: PATH OF AWAKENING: KEYS FOR TRANSFIGURATION is an in-depth collection of spiritual and philosophical wisdom to support personal, relational, and planetary healing. If you are in the beginning stages of awakening or moving through a deep healing process, you may wish to start here so you can develop your consciousness and prepare your mind and body for higher level initiation into the Mysteries.

GATEWAY FOUR: CHAKRA YOGA DISCOURSE transmits deeper

insight into the themes and physio-psycho-spiritual domains of the vortices of life force and perception called the *chakras*. Each section transmits valuable information to understand the common distortions in these processing centers and how to activate ard reconcile each center.

GATEWAY FIVE: LAYING HANDS: REIKI & BEYOND is a full manual for learning the art of the laying of hands for healing. The manual clearly describes all the stages, steps, and practices to perform powerfully transformative hands-on-healing sessions for yourself, others, and even in groups. This manual would be acceptable for any Level 1 and Level 2 Reiki course.

GATEWAY SIX: ASCENSION LEXICON is a glossary of commonly used words to describe the process of awakening and ascension. These definitions act as keycode activators to unlock deeper meaning and inner wisdom. Many words used in spiritual/ascension circles are convoluted and sometimes lose their impact because they are misused or misunderstood. I may use words in a way you are not familiar with, or I may use words differently than you. I tried my best to make a glossary with foundational vocabulary to assist with understanding the material. You may wish to read the ASCENSION LEXICON before journeying through the main text of the book.

Bless you on your personal path through this material. May the light in your heart guide you with ease and grace on your journey of initiation with *The Illumination Codex*.

Awakening to the Quantum Reality

In the Summer of 2016, I was given a book that forever changed my life's direction called *The Three Waves of Volunteers and the New Earth* by Dolores Cannon. This book was a huge catalyst in my spiritual awakening. Reading the text stirred something deep within me and resonated profoundly with my heart's truth. The book's pages sent waves of energy down my spine as I began to awaken to a higher consciousness reality and remember my purpose for being born upon the Earth at this time.

Dolores Cannon was a world-renowned hypnotherapist specializing in past-life regression. To understand the power of regressive hypnosis, we also need to understand the workings of the mind. The mind can be separated into three categories: the conscious mind, the subconscious mind, and the superconscious mind.

The conscious mind is the ego/personality part of the mind. This active part of the mind uses limited information from the environment and past experiences to make decisions and take care of the body.

The subconscious mind is the recording device of our mind. It records incredible amounts of information at every moment. We easily pull data from the subconscious when we think about something from our past as we access memory.

Deeper in the subconscious, sometimes called the unconscious mind, we have unconscious memories and information, including societal conditioning, painful traumas from this life that are too painful to remember, and memories from other lifetimes. Even though this information is not in the conscious mind, it silently influences our day-to-day experience as reactive emotional momentum, called *samskaras* in Sanskrit, from past events which overlay and filter our experience of the present moment. These subconscious patterns are like applications running in the background of smartphones that quietly drain the processing speed and battery, silently influencing processor speed and functionality.

The superconscious mind is a higher mind capacity that gives us access to intuitive information, extrasensory perception, non-local consciousness, creative genius, universal connection, and access to divine consciousness. This part of the mind is mostly undiscovered and underdeveloped in most of humanity.

Dolores created a unique method of hypnosis, Quantum Healing Hypnosis Technique (QHHT), that opened a doorway to the client's subconscious mind to explore other lifetimes and realms in Creation. When I use the word "quantum," I am speaking to the fabric of Consciousness, the multidimensional unified field of Creation. When clients are in these hypnotic states, they tap into the part of their consciousness that is nonlocal and connected to All That Is. This includes access to other lifetimes, other realities and dimensions, and other intelligent consciousness forms (i.e., higher-dimensional light beings, telepathic extraterrestrials, etc.). Through this experience, clients came to understand another perspective and origin of self-sabotaging and limiting beliefs that were playing out in this life and the core mental/emotional patterns that create illness and disease.

During her sessions, Dolores started to contact a part of her clients' consciousness that seemed to have endless knowledge and wisdom. She called this aspect of her clients the Subconscious or the SC. Others have called this the Higher Self, the oversoul, superconsciousness, or the cosmic consciousness. I prefer the term Higher Self and superconscious mind and go into great detail of how to activate and evolve superconsciousness throughout this text. While the information was limitless, the SC/Higher Self would only answer questions in a way that was appropriate for the client's learning path and honored their free will. When working with the SC, both Dolores and the client described powerful healing energy in their bodies and the treatment room. Clients often reported instantaneous healing as they were transformed from the inside out during the session. While this may seem too good to be true, there are countless documented and measurable occurrences where clients received lasting miraculous healing through these types of sessions.

When she would work with the Higher Self, this higher consciousness identity and supportive Light team would speak through the client as a collective consciousness as if the client were speaking in third-person perspective about themselves. "We are always guiding her. We wish she would follow her intuition more." and "We are beginning to use white light to heal this now." are common examples of how "They" (i.e., SC/Higher Self) express themselves and heal the client during the session.

The healing work is always done with unconditional love and honors the free will and sovereignty of the client. If instantaneous healing was not "appropriate" for the client's growth and spiritual maturation, "They" would suggest what steps the client should take to heal themself. Slowly, over many years, Dolores's work expanded as "They" introduced more components to the healing process so that she could evolve her work and teach it to others.

The Three Waves of Volunteers and the New Earth was one of nineteen books written by Dolores Cannon before her transition out of physical life. Each book contains transcriptions of client sessions describing detailed events from other lives while using her Quantum Healing Hypnosis Technique (QHHT).

Awakening to the Starseed Volunteer Mission

After several years of working with clients worldwide, Dolores noticed a pattern of clients describing a massive galactic and higher dimensional mission to raise the vibration of the planet and shift it into a new reality called the New Earth. The book describes how countless numbers of advanced spiritual beings from distant star systems, and even other universes, volunteered to incarnate on the Earth with a mission to raise consciousness on the planet and assist with this grand transition.

The New Earth is a higher frequency Earth reality that exists in a higher dimension than we are in now. Clients describe a large-scale plan initiated by Source Intelligence (God) to reset life on planet Earth back to the original template of a harmonic environment thriving within diversity. Parallel to this, Dolores's work described a shift in human consciousness from a duality-based mindset to a heart-centered, multidimensional consciousness and a less physical body of light.

The First Wave Volunteers were born beginning around 1945 through the 1970s. They were like a stealthy reconnaissance mission. First on the scene. First to patrol and feel out the collective consciousness vibrations. First to introduce the higher consciousness perspectives to the masses. Many had a difficult and lonely time since there were not many other humans in higher, love-based spiritual consciousness on the planet at the time.

The Second Wave Volunteers were born around the late 1970s through

1990s and are channels for higher spiritual energy and divine wisdom. These souls came in with a higher level of intuitive gifts and are often extremely sensitive to energy. Many are hands-on healers, musicians, vocalists, yoga teachers, and so on. They are space-holders who transmit a new frequency out to the field of Earth, bridging the old ways with the new ways and consciousness of New Earth.

The Third Wave Volunteers, the younger generations, are builders and innovative geniuses in science, spirituality, technology, and so on. They are divinely inspired visionaries that will build the New Earth. They are radical lovers and shine bright with crystalline eyes and have achieved high consciousness levels in other lifetimes. Some of these souls have never had a physical incarnation or have come straight from Source as new souls with pure Light and no karma.

I have been told all the children born at this time are part of this Grand Mission. They are pure souls, evolutionary masters, here to build the New Earth. More is written about the Starseed Mission and phenomena later in this book.

As I was reading Dolores's book, I felt I was reading my own story. I felt the truth in her words. Suddenly so many things made sense about my life. I finally had answers to why I felt so different from others in my community and family. I understood why I felt other people's emotions and could tell what people were thinking. It all started to click together. I was so excited to share the book with Ron, my husband and co-founder of New Earth Ascending, who also deeply resonated with the material.

At the same time, we were beginning to work with an Australian musical group as dancers for their "Return of the Bird Tribes" tour for their album by the same name. Something about the term "bird tribes" caught my attention, and I started to research it. I found the book by the same name, written by Ken Carey, in 1988 that describes a prophecy of high spiritual beings returning to the Earth at a time of spiritual renewal.

Many cultures describe times when culture-bringing beings would come from the heavens or from across the waters to bring technology and information to humanity throughout history. Thoth went to the Egyptians, White Buffalo Calf Woman went to the Native Americans, Quetzalcoatl went to the Aztecs, the Seven Sisters of the Pleiades went to the Aboriginal people of Australia, beings from the Sirius A and B binary star system went to the Dogon people of Mali; and many other stories exist in many other cultures. Carey's book described when these beings would come again during a time of spiritual awakening on the planet.

I was receiving information from multiple directions and was going through a massive realignment with my soul's purpose as I became aware of this greater story and mission. Ron and I went to an arts festival in the desert of Nevada called Burning Man. While we were there, a couple excitedly recognized us as "twin flames" and asked us which star system we had come from. "We are from Sirius. Where are you from? Orion? The Pleiades? Sirius?" she asked. The concept of "starseeds" and "twin flames" was new to me, and I did not know what to say. I saw a special sparkle in the couple's eyes and felt that I should do some research to understand more about it.

After some research and some magical synchronicities, Ron convinced me that we should do the QHHT training and certification process. I was super resistant to learning it because of deep religious programming and egoic structures that made me doubtful of the truthfulness of the work. I was familiar with reincarnation but did not necessarily believe in it. Eventually, I gave in to Ron's suggestion and took the QHHT course.

Evolving Beyond QHHT

In the early stages of practicing QHHT, Ron and I were guided to start doing the sessions online to share the technique's power with as many people as we could. This method was not permitted by the organization because Dolores did not believe it to be safe and her organization does not permit it still. Dolores was an elder and this type of technology was new to her, whereas the younger generations are much more comfortable interfacing with video conferencing.

We have been told by the Higher Consciousness that there is nothing to fear, and NOW is the time to spread these healing methods across the world in whatever way is possible. To honor our lineage and teacher, we stopped using the name QHHT and started experimenting with different names as our way of practicing quantum healing evolved beyond our initial training.

Online sessions are just as powerful as in-person sessions and are often more comfortable and affordable for the client. It is completely safe to facilitate sessions remotely, and we have had countless powerful sessions that have been facilitated in this way. Dolores's organization does not allow adaptation of the QHHT technique. Its practitioners need to perform the method exactly how Dolores taught and not add any modifications or outside techniques. While it is important to protect the work's integrity, this rigidity does not permit the work to expand to its full potential. We are in a time of expansion and evolution, and we must always be open to the transformation and progression of all methods we currently use or risk leaving them in the past as everything on the Earth is evolving.

Another topic that caused us to evolve beyond our initial training of QHHT was the organization's strict denial of negative spiritual attachment and what felt like shaming those who believed in this common experience. Ron and I and other quantum healing practitioners discovered that certain psychological, emotional, and physical imbalances were being created by pervasive energies that did not belong to the client's energy field that had somehow become attached to the client. This includes spirit attachments, curses from past lives, and implants from nefarious beings to name a few. QHHT did not provide us with appropriate training to work with these serious complications. If it were found out that a practitioner had adopted these practices and still operated under the name of QHHT, practitioners could be removed from the QHHT directory.

Many practitioners have reported spontaneous visitation from Dolores through clients under hypnosis where she has encouraged practitioners to follow their intuitive guidance and continue to develop the work through experimentation just as she did when she developed QHHT.

We were inspired greatly by other quantum healing practitioners' extraction methods and crafted our own approaches to clearing pervasive energies and spirit attachments. The reality of negative thought-forms, negative extraterrestrial implants, and entity attachment is too big to ignore, considering so many cases are emerging, not to forget the thousands of years of wisdom and extraction practices passed down by Indigenous peoples and various wisdom traditions.

We never assume that someone has an entity just because they suffer, and we do not bring it up in our intake interview. Once the client is deep in a hypnotic trance, we ask the Higher Self if there are entities or attached energies. If the answer is yes, then we ask questions to understand how this occurred and if the client has anything to learn to release negative attachment. From there, the Higher Self can immediately extract the energy and take it back into the Light for healing. It is all extremely safe, insightful, and benefits all who are involved. We have found that, often, the revelation of spirit attachment or implants will not occur unless the practitioner asks and gives permission for a scan specifically for attached energies. Ron and I believe this is because of the honoring of the free will of the entities involved in the experience of attachment.

In my opinion, to continue to deny such experiences is a disservice to the clients who come to us seeking answers and healing. All practices and traditions can become dogmatic if we do not allow the evolution of thought to take us into new frontiers of consciousness. These are evolutionary practices, and we need to be constantly open to shifting our paradigm so that we can offer the best guidance and support with the changing of times.

Once we started offering quantum healing sessions online, clients started coming to Ron and me from all over the world. Not only were the sessions powerfully healing and transformative for the clients, but we were also going through a rapid transformation as we learned about ancient stories and galactic events from the perspective of souls embodied at those times. While Dolores taught that many people had "potato-picking lives," simple lives with simple themes, it seemed that almost every session of mine had to do with the New Earth Mission, powerful events from the ancient past, and future timelines of Earth.

I soon realized that I was getting a theme and timeline in my sessions. The timeline given to me via my clients describes how Creation came into being, ancient galactic history, the seeding of life on Earth, the rise and fall of ancient civilizations, the true teachings of Jesus through the eyes of people that were closest to him, information about the transformation of the human body to a less dense body of Light, and the evolution of the Earth into the higher frequency reality of New Earth. In less than a year, I went from a reincarnation skeptic to believing that anything is possible, and that the multiverse is more incredible than we can even imagine!

Illuminated Quantum Healing

After years of practicing and evolving how we do this work, Ron and I have created our own quantum healing method that incorporates all that we have learned on our path. This includes facilitating sessions online to reach as many people as possible to assist in this Great Awakening.

Our training method acknowledges spirit attachment and teaches our facilitators how to perform negative spirit releasement. We teach yogic psychology, holistic wellness concepts, and energy healing methods to ensure the practitioner has a thorough understanding of human consciousness and how to lead the client through the ascension process using multiple IQH sessions and mentorship programs. We call our method Illuminated Quantum Healing. IQH can be learned in live classes or through our online course offered on our social network Source◉Energy.

Illuminated Quantum Healing (IQH) is a personal transformation method for multidimensional holistic healing and consciousness development. IQH incorporates energy healing, meditative practices, yogic philosophy, and hypnosis skills to reconcile limiting subconscious patterning and integrate instantaneous multidimensional healing and wisdom from one's Higher Self.

I am deeply honored to be a part of this work. I am so blessed to have an opportunity to work with such incredible people and energies. Each session that I facilitate nourishes me to the core, and I have the sublime opportunity to observe miraculous instantaneous healing and transformation in my clients. After witnessing the infinite potential of quantum healing hypnosis, I firmly believe that we can ascend beyond all states of illness and disease and that we have infinite support to move beyond the shadows of our past and become a new People of Light.

Getting to the New Earth involves a process of spiritual growth and purification. To transition with the Earth, it is required that we raise our vibration to match the accelerating frequency of the Earth as it changes. Mostly, this is about releasing fear and negative karma. I have written this book as a tool to use for your spiritual awakening and transformation that many are calling Ascension. This is my gift to humanity to help make the process easier and explain different components to cultivate a deeper understanding of this Grand Shift to New Earth and our newly evolving Lightbody.

Spiritual awakening and ascension are available for ALL people no matter what they have done in their past, current economic status, gender expression, sexuality, religion, etc. There are as many paths to the New Earth as there are humans on the planet. No one religion holds the keys or the way to heaven. The power is within YOU!

To support the global ascension process, we have created New Earth Ascending. New Earth Ascending is a non-profit, faith-based organization focused on global ascension and establishing heart-centered, sustainable communities and educational centers around the world.

Alongside Illuminated Quantum Healing (IQH), Ron and I have created other pathways of support for the global ascension process:

1. Embodied Light Reiki Training and Certification
2. New Earth Ascending has three levels of Reiki certification to train people how to channel divine light for healing. These trainings honor the lineage and teachings of the Usui System of Natural Healing while also infusing evolutionary concepts and practices that go beyond standard Reiki training.
3. Online courses for awakening and ascension are available on our private social network Source⊙Energy. The courses include philosophical exploration on several models of spiritual growth and alchemical practices to support your healing, awakening, and ascension. These courses include meditations, holistic wellness education, breathwork, lightbody activation and more. These courses lay foundational understanding for beginners and move through a progression of intermediate and advanced practices and knowledge.
4. TransformOtion was created to support the embodiment of one's Higher Self using dance, somatic movement, yogic practices, meditation, imagination, and energy healing. This fusion of practices helps to purify and repair the physical, etheric, and mental bodies so that one can move beyond perceived limitations into boundless rhythm and flow. Through this interweaving of multiple disciplinary paths, we integrate physicality with transcendental ecstatic play while cultivating a deep connection with and trust in the body's wisdom.

These ideas and concepts can be used for personal embodiment and activation or infused into performance art to create powerful alchemical experiences for the performer and the audience. This fusion of high art and spiritual transformation creates a multidimensional experience for all who are within the field of performance energies.

5. Source⊙Energy is a social network exclusively for those on the path of ascension to connect and share inspiration as we manifest and build a New Earth. We invite all souls who feel aligned with New Earth to join this network and add your unique energy and love to this community. Source⊙Energy serves as a pathway of social interaction and is the home of our online courses and training.

6. Children are our future. Youth inspiration and enrichment programming is in development to assist the spiritual activation and consciousness mastery of the youth. NEA is dedicated to creating harmonic environments and rich educational programs to guide youth to connect with cosmic intelligence and embody their divine nature and mastery as they build the New Earth.

Ron and I have dedicated our lives to supporting this Grand Transition. We stand alongside all of you as humanity awakens to its True Nature and becomes a People of Light in the heavenly reality of New Earth.

New Earth Ascending is dedicated to assisting people to realize their divinity and manifest that truth in every aspect of their life. For more information about New Earth Ascending or to contact Michael, please scan the QR code below for a list of resources and links, or visit *www.newearthascending.org*. Be sure to check out our courses including the Illuminated Quantum Healing practitioner course.

New Earth Ascending is a registered 508 (c)(1)(a) Self-Supported Non-profit Church Ministry with a global outreach. We greatly appreciate your support as we create new systems, communities, and schools for the development of the New Earth civilization. If you would like to make a tax-deductible donation to support our mission, please go to:

https://donorbox.org/donationtonewearthascending

Scan with a smart device camera for more information!

NEW EARTH ASCENDING
VISIONARY CREED

We acknowledge the sovereignty and equality of all levels of Creation and support the liberation of all of Life from cycles of suffering. We believe in the power of divine sovereign creatorship endowed to us by God/Source and dedicate our life to Light and Love in service to All. We believe in conscious participation, empowering everyone to activate awakening in themselves and their community.

We recognize free will and surrender our will and desires to the higher will of the Divine. We believe in divine timing and practice trust, patience, and tolerance as we witness the unfoldment of the perfection of the Divine Plan. We believe in the potency of empowering prayer, meditation, and ritual as tools for communication with the Divine for the culmination of spiritual light and divine wisdom. We believe everyone has a direct connection to the Source and no intermediary is needed. When we come together in fellowship, prayer, and devotion, we amplify the light of each individuals' loving intention through our unified, heart-centered consciousness.

We seek to uplift all groups and communities so that we may celebrate our unity, diversity, and wholeness. New Earth Ascending is non-competitive and embraces an ecumenical relationship with all religions and wisdom traditions. We believe in interfaith and inter-spirituality, acknowledging the teachings of Light, Love, and Wisdom in many traditions, philosophies, and cultures. We believe that no single religion holds the keys to the Kingdom of God and the blessings of redemption are available to all people through their unbreakable innate connection to the Godhead.

We believe in the Law of Oneness and that all of Creation emanates from one Divine Source that has both masculine and feminine principles. As we heal and balance the divine masculine and divine feminine principles within us, we embody the divine androgyny of Source and Nature as a harmonic synthesis of Spirit and Matter.

We believe that humanity and planet Earth are going through a rapid physical and spiritual transformation called by many as The Ascension or The Event. We believe this process to be part of a higher evolutionary divine plan guided by the Source of Creation and legions of beings working for the Light. This evolutionary process is multidimensional and is beyond the standard biological evolution spoken of by modern science.

We believe that we, as humanity, are awakening to our spiritual Self and are becoming a heart-based, unity-focused species with higher, multidimensional awareness, which some call Christ Consciousness, Cosmic Consciousness, or 5D Consciousness. We believe this transformation's power is happening through our divinely designed and curated DNA as the physical body transforms into a less dense body of Light with tremendously expanded multidimensional abilities.

We believe that Planet Earth, the sentient being of Gaia, is going through a similar restoration process and will soon transform into a revitalized higher dimensional planet, which many are calling the New Earth. Earth changes, weather events, crumbling institutional structures, frequency fluctuations, and astrological phenomena are all signs that we are nearing that shift into the next Golden Age, where Heaven and Earth become one and all systems of control and limitation will fall away.

We believe that we are supported by benevolent higher dimensional, subterranean, and extraterrestrial beings that work in harmonic collaboration with the higher evolutionary Divine Plan of Source. We believe that soon humanity will be consciously reunited with these benevolent beings and serve the higher evolutionary plan of the Light and Love of Source as cosmic co-citizens of the Multiverse working as one Family of Light in service to all of Creation.

We understand that the pathway of Self/Source-Realization and Ascension is comprised of self-study, self-practice, self-discipline, and steadfastness. We practice self-care and self-purification to clarify our Light. We acknowledge and value the acceleration of this process when we practice together in groupings of two or more in fellowship and worship.

We strive to grow in awareness and focused attention, practicing mindfulness in all areas of our lives to grow as conscious, heart-centered creators. We choose to focus our life positively with faith and knowing that Life is evolving in perfection following the Divine Plan of the Supreme Source.

We believe in the power of intention. We practice nonviolence and non-harmfulness in intention, thought, and action. We strive to release all forms of judgment and dual thinking. We honor the sacred heart's radiant potential and believe loving compassion and understanding to be The Way. We practice the heart-centered qualities of gentleness, reverence, loving-kindness, and forgiveness as pathways to reconciliation to emulate the eternal grace of Source and our Earth Mother, Gaia.

We see that Truth is alive within each of us, and we practice inner reflection to grow in discernment for what energies are resonant with our inner Source and our path. We practice benevolent truthfulness, honesty, straightforwardness, and vulnerability to embody and vocalize our deepest truth.

We value and practice transparency and accountability, believing in the opportunity for spiritual growth through spiritual partnership with our community members. We recognize one another as divine mirrors, reflecting to us where we are in our vibration, beliefs, and intentions.

We practice sacred sexuality as an alchemical tool for Divine Union and Ascension. We strive to purify our intentions and desires to align with Higher Love and authentic connection. We believe in heart-based self and consensual mutual pleasure to unite body, mind, and spirit so that we may deepen in our love and authentic connection to our Divine Self, our partner(s), and Creation.

We practice contentment, acceptance, appreciation, and gratitude for our life's many blessings and lessons. We practice non-attachment, non-possessiveness, non-stealing, non-excess, and sustainability, for all we need is given to us through our alignment with our Creator Source and our connection to our Earth Mother. We practice stewardship and sustainable selfless service, acknowledging our responsibility to take care of the world around us and within.

We practice sacred commerce, investing our resources, time, and energy towards the greater good and sustainability of our community and planet. We believe in reciprocal energy exchange and strive to do so when able. We practice generosity, hospitality, and charitability as reflections of the abundance of the Universe.

We strive to embody and emulate these spiritual principles to manifest the complete liberation of all beings from cycles of suffering and to assist this Grand Transition into the New Earth.

Bless us all!

Gateway Two Part Three: New Earth Transmissions

Future Timelines of Gaia

ONE

The Shift of the Ages

Humanity stands at the brink of unprecedented transformation, a gigantic quantum leap in consciousness that has been foretold by many prophets in many cultures throughout history. This is the Omega phase, the ending of a grand experimental cycle where all the karma of Earth and humanity will be reconciled as the Earth is transformed into a higher light spectrum reality commonly known as the New Earth. In unison, humanity is going through its own transformation process to become a civilization of Light, divine beings in sophisticated bodies of Light who operate from a liberated and expanded multidimensional consciousness.

Ascension was brought into the collective consciousness of humanity through the teachings of Christ Jesus, also known as Yeshua ben Joseph, the Master of Light for Planet Earth. This rapid transformation process is supported by leagues of benevolent extraterrestrial and ultraterrestrial beings that form a Hierarchy of Light that serves a higher evolution following a Divine Plan established by the Source of Creation. As humanity and Earth ascends, we will be consciously reunited with the Hierarchy of Light and the Star Nations and live as cooperative cosmic citizens united in a higher consciousness reality.

In my attempt to describe the indescribable, I will mostly refer to the Supreme Consciousness and all its functions as the Source of Creation or simply Source. For me, this term accurately describes what many commonly call God. Some traditions have different names for Source in pre-manifestation such as *Ein Soph* or *Brahman* and another term for God with manifested attributes like *Ein Soph Or, Ishvara*, or *Logos*. For simplicity, I will simply use the term Source to speak for both the transcendental and manifested expressions of the Supreme Consciousness. Many people have turned their backs on the Divine and religious institutions because of the pain and suffering created by dogma, sexual abuse, hypocrisy, religious wars, and oppression. Each person carries a unique definition and set of internal images and emotions evoked by the word "God." While some people believe in a higher power of some kind, others reject the idea of a god-man in the clouds punishing and judging the world for their sins. Some can at least recognize some type of higher connection to nature. Some have decided to have nothing to do with spirituality and the divine and choose to stick with modern versions of science and what they can sense through their five senses.

The dualistic philosophy of Samkhya speaks of Source in terms of *Purusha* and *Prakriti*. *Purusha* is the pure consciousness, the Seer of Creation. *Purusha* in the human is the Self, the *Atman*, the pure Source within that observes this bodymind and this universe. *Prakriti*, Sanskrit for Nature or Creation, is everything in manifestation, everything with a name and form. This includes all universes, all dimensions and realities including the higher "heavenly" light dimensions, and our concept of God.

Prakriti can also be called *maya*, a Sanskrit term commonly translated as illusion or magic. Source through its power of *maya* projects this entire universe including the bodymind complex you find yourself in. When people say only Source is real and everything else is false, an illusion, it is because all names and forms borrow existence from the Eternal Source, the Pure Consciousness that you truly are.

Maya not only projects names and forms into creation but it also veils the True Reality. A classic example of the power of *maya* is when a person sees a rope out of the corner of their eye and mistakenly thinks it is a snake. *Maya* has veiled the true nature of the rope, so one sees a snake. At the most fundamental level, the Absolute level, neither the snake no the rope exists. It is Source using its power of maya to project a whole reality which includes the rope which one confuses as a snake, a dream within a dream, within a dream.

Another classic example of this is water which comes in many names and forms. Whether we call it an ocean, a glacier, fog, or mist it is all water. All these objects with different names and forms borrow existence from the water. In the same way, all is Source appearing as universes, planets, individual plants, animals, good people, evil people, energy, and emotion. Yet all of it borrows existence from Source, the pure Consciousness which you are.

One of the purposes of *Prakriti*, of *maya,* is to test the Seer's ability to perceive the True Source that is behind all manifestations. *Maya* arises, abides, and dissolves in an ever-changing landscape pulling our senses and awareness in every direction. *Maya* seduces us and ensnares our consciousness in the pull of sensory experiences and deepens our misidentification with our bodymind, distracting our attention from our True Nature. We falsely believe that all we see, touch, taste, smell, feel, and think is real and become enamored by the dream of reality, overlooking our True Nature. It is a game we play with our Oneself. A game of forgetting and remembering who we truly are as Pure Consciousness.

Our perceived reality is like a distorted funhouse mirror that bends, shrinks, and accentuates the reflected image. The thing with a funhouse mirror is that most people can keep the awareness that what they are seeing is not real. In a physical body, it is much harder to stay aware that only Source is the true reality and that all the rest is smoke and mirrors. It is our own complex inner reality that is projected and outpictured, distorting and hypnotizing our mind into emotional intoxication and spiritual amnesia.

In physical life, the initiate is tested in their ability to stay laser-focused on the true reality of Divine Love in the background of all experiences and to invite what is normally in the background of experience into the foreground so that the "face of God" is all that one perceives.

Sometimes in my hypnosis sessions, a client returns to the Source. Typically, they describe the environment as being a bright warm light and that they feel so loved. They say that many other beings are there and that everything feels so good there. Sometimes they say something like, "We are many, but we are all one." I ask them how long they have been there, and they often respond with something like "There is no time here." or "What do you mean? We have always been here." I usually let the client experience this for a few minutes to deeply remember the love they came from and truly are. Often clients are crying tears of joy as years of trauma and struggle begin to melt away through the power of union with Source. It is a powerful and beautiful thing to witness.

Interfaith dialogue recognizes the threads of harmonic commonality found in religious and spiritual texts, philosophy, humanitarian beliefs, and science. As humanity awakens, many realize that there is a common foundation in all these traditions and viewpoints of what "God" is and the meaning of Life.

As we move forward on the New Earth timeline, we can release our wounds from religious dogma and be open to the teachings of Light and

Unconditional Love inherently found within the sacred texts from ancient cultures and world traditions. We can drop the dogma of dead religions focused on fear and condemnation and find the indwelling of the Living Source Within and claim our divine inheritance.

When I speak of Creation, I am speaking of the holographic Multiverse. The Multiverse has been described by several different mystical philosophies and esoteric wisdom traditions using different terms to describe the various planes and subplanes of reality. They all seem to agree on one plane that is the substratum of all the other planes, the plane of the Absolute, Source, or God. From this Absolute Reality all other planes and subplanes emerge. Another level of reality is the Transactional Reality of Relativity, the realm of phenomenon where the Light of Consciousness interacts in different forms with varying frequencies and polarizations interacting in varying planes of light density. This level would include the physical plane we are in and the higher experimental light dimensions. Another level is the Reality of Illusion such as mirages or the reality we experience in our dream states which appears real until we are in our waking consciousness.

Just like in lucid dreaming where the Dreamer awakens in the dream, another level of awakening can happen during our waking consciousness. When the soul is ready, spiritual consciousness begins to stir awake and higher knowledge leads their consciousness out of entanglement with the Transactional Reality towards the realization of the Ultimate Reality which is both imminent and transcendent. God-Source is both beyond the knowable universe and the Universal Principle which pervades all realities, realms, planes, and dimensions. This is what Christ meant when he said to go within to find the Kingdom of God. All that you seek is already within, yet you must seek it to find it.

All of Creation exists within a continuum of ascending and descending movement patterning to and from the Source. Divine Light flows from this Source out into many levels and layers of Creation, universes within universes, existing in various states of light density. Within these multidimensional experimental zones of Light exist a multitude of species, physical and nonphysical, in various states of evolution with each plane of Creation working in symbiotic relationship within a unified field of Source Consciousness. As the light descends in frequency, we arrive at the physical dimension, the material plane that our universe exists in. Light descends from the higher dimensions and is projected through one Great Central Sun of this universe which pulses evolutionary coding through a vast stellar "modem" network of fixed stars. Each Central Sun broadcasts multidimensional light coding to evolve each "theater of evolution" in accordance with the higher plan of the Divine.

Eventually, we arrive at our Sun, the central star of our solar system, which emanates all the intelligent coding for the evolution of countless levels of life forms and celestial bodies in our solar system. Even each planet in our solar system is connected through a web of subtle energy pathways that support the other celestial bodies. Everything, including each individual human, is connected within this web of evolutionary communication and complex multidimensional configuration.

At the beginning of Creation, the Divine Intelligence sent out parts of its Oneself to create, learn, and explore. When I use the word "soul," I am speaking of the individual lightbody essence, the conglomerate of subtle bodies, that has been sent into the realms of Creation to learn and create with free will. This part takes on lessons and karma as a way of learning and growing as it ascends back towards the realization of its true origin and true nature which I refer to as the Source within, the Atman, the Witness, or pure Consciousness.

The soul is immortal, has lived many incarnations, and will release the physical body upon its death experience and continue its evolutionary journey in other forms. The soul is a portion of what I call the oversoul, which is a higher density form of your consciousness that exists beyond this physical dimension of reality which you will be consciously reconnected with as we shift into the fifth dimensional (5D) also called 4th Density, New Earth reality. The oversoul is like a quantum information storehouse of all the information collected from all of its many soul aspects which have lived myriad lifetimes throughout eternity.

The Hindu traditions describe the journey of ascension as *jiva* (personal self) as it awakens to Atman (Source within) or Brahman (God/Source), experienced as Eternal Existence, Eternal Consciousness, and Eternal Bliss. The Kabbalistic/Jewish traditions describe it at the journey of the *Nephesh* (soul) that is matured into *Neshamah* (sovereign soul or Spirit-soul Synthesis) through the ministering Spirit (*Ruach*). The Buddhists describe it as an awakening to the Buddha within. The Hare Krishnas describe it as the path to Krishnahood or Krishna Consciousness. The Christians call it being "saved" and following the path of Christ. The New Age community calls it ascending to Christ Consciousness. Each of these beautiful traditions and philosophies describes the same ascension process and the same spark of the Creator within all of us that has taken on karma to learn and grow through a process of God-Realization.

While there may be differences in practices or conflicting philosophies in some of these traditions, there is a beautiful interweaving of them all that can give us keys and insight into the greater tapestry of Creation. There are infinite philosophies, infinite practices of devotion, and infinite pathways of Ascension back to the Source. All of these wisdom traditions lead to the same Source, the same Love, the same Light. If you are reading this text, you can rest assured that you are on your unique path of Ascension.

Throughout this book, I will speak of intention and consciousness in terms of service-to-self negative polarity (STS), and service-to-all (STA), positive polarity, which some call service-to-others (STO). Religions speak of "good" and "evil" with a charge of judgment. The problem is everyone has a different definition of what those terms mean.

Service-to-self (STS) consciousness is when we serve our false self, our ego, often at the expense of others. The negative polarity in our consciousness is all about me, me, me! Individuals in the negative polarity are concerned with self-preservation and the accumulation of external power. Negatively polarized consciousness manifests as passive aggression, selfishness, greed, pride, domination, control, egoism, and so on. Individuals and groups that are negatively polarized are often also called "dark," "evil," or tyrannical as the fullest expression of negative polarity is consciousness cemented fully in material reality and is void of higher spiritual intelligence and empathy.

Service-to-all (STA) consciousness is a mindset of honoring and protecting the expansion, freedom, and joy of the world around you while respecting your own inner being, sovereignty, and alignment. Positively polarized consciousness manifests as gentleness, benevolent truth speaking, healthy boundaries, forgiveness, devotion, and all other attitudes and actions of harmony and stewardship. People holding a high level of positive polarity consistently act altruistically and from a place of loving compassion and spiritual unity. Individuals and groups from the positive polarity are often called "good," "holy," and "light," as they reflect the benevolence and goodness of the Divine.

This concept speaks to something deeper than action and points to the underlying intention that drives thought, speech, and action. Someone may appear to be positively polarized, service-to-all, but in actuality is using nicety to manipulate others or protect their ego-self. Conversely, someone may be judged as "negative" because they say something that stirs up chaos but, in actuality, are doing so because of their commitment to truth and goodness. Look at what happened to Jesus. Even as "the world" projected hatred and judgment on him, his actions were for goodwill.

We all hold consciousness that is of both sides of polarity. As we begin to awaken, we begin to transform our negative polarity into positive polarity by aligning with our deepest truth and the unity of the compassionate heart. We move from an STS, negatively polarized, expression into an STA, positively polarized embodiment of righteousness, unconditional love, and spiritual sovereignty.

Earth has been an experimental zone for the full spectrum of thought, from the evilest and most negatively polarized to the most sublime and pure expressions of consciousness. That experiment is ending as the negative polarity, the service-to-self consciousness thought-forms, will no longer be permitted in the New Earth reality. So now we see all of those ways we have hidden from our True Nature coming to the surface to be reconciled by compassion and noble action. Those shifting to the 5D New Earth consciousness are those who are making the polarity switch and raising their overall vibration. Truly, unconditional love and unity consciousness is the way to the New Earth.

The Event

For some time now, highly charged photonic waves have been broadcasting from the Great Central Sun of our universe, pulsating from central sun to central sun carrying streams of divinely encoded evolutionary energies that are revitalizing and renewing all that they touch. These Light information pulsations are awakening the consciousness of humanity from the duality of polarized consciousness towards the awakened and liberated higher consciousness that many are calling christ consciousness, cosmic consciousness, or oversoul consciousness. Christ consciousness is not only for those of a mainstream religion. This consciousness is available to all people who choose to live a life of unconditional love and unity. It is the pure Light consciousness of the Universe, and it is your birthright to realize this capacity in yourself as a liberated being of Light.

Space Weather and the Schumann Resonance

Some of these evolutionary energy events are being picked up with modern technology. Solar events like solar wind, coronal mass ejections, and solar flares bring major upgrades to the planet. I have noticed that when the solar wind reaches 400 km/sec, I start having headaches, chest tension, dehydration, and emotional sensitivity. The higher the solar wind speed, the more amplified these symptoms are. When solar wind speed reaches 600 km/sec or higher, I am either wiped out, emotional, need lots of water, or I feel like I am riding a wave of bliss and insight. Everyone handles these energy waves differently and there are simple self-care practices and protocols that you can implement to help the integration process. These are mentioned later in the book.

Another measurement to watch is the Schumann Resonance. The Schumann Resonance measures Earth's atmosphere's electromagnetic frequencies found in the cavity between Earth's surface and the ionosphere. The lowest frequency mode and fundamental Schumann Resonance is 7.83 Hz, followed by harmonics of 14 Hz, 20 Hz, 26 Hz, 33 Hz, 39 Hz, and 45 Hz (rounded numbers for the sake of simplicity). It has been found that when the wave size or amplitude of these frequencies increases, we may experience direct effects on our electromagnetic fields causing fluctuations in our emotions, cognition, cardiac system, and consciousness. I have been following an online Schumann Resonance monitor associated with the Tomsk State University in Tomsk, Russia for the last few years. I have noticed a direct relationship between fluctuations of the Earth's frequencies and my own mental, emotional, etheric, and physical experiences that I call ascension symptoms.

It should be noted that sensitive people worldwide also report "ascension symptoms" even when the measurable frequencies (space weather and Schumann) are not present. I believe that these energies are coming from a source that humanity does not have measurement technologies for at the time. This can include friendly spacecraft, distant planets and stars, and other sources, including the Photon Belt. Earth will be passing through the Photon Belt for around another 2,000 years, which will dramatically accelerate the ascension processes. These light waves are building in intensity and potency gradually changing all of life as we know it on the planet.

We cannot even imagine the world we are about to awaken to from our current consciousness level. Each wave awakens another group of souls on the New Earth trajectory and begins their healing, activation, and divine embodiment process. Those who have awakened before the rest of humanity will experience "The Event" as a series of waves and upgrading energies that gradually lead us into higher and higher consciousness. For others, they will continue in the lower dimensional consciousness until they experience a wave that awakens them to their higher consciousness as the planet makes its ascension into the New Earth reality. All of this was designed pre-incarnation and we are watching the timings play out.

There are many people who build up a lot of emotion expecting a major solar event that instantly awakens and changes the Earth. This may or may not happen as the many timelines and probabilities play out. In some ways, the Solar Flash has become a "savior program" for many. In truth, all experiences arise within the Light of our own Self. We are the Solar Flash! We are the Divine Plan in action!

After these energy waves leave the Sun, they make contact with the biofield/aura of Earth. After the energy passes through the Earth's electromagnetic fields, the energies enter our biofield and begin to enter the tissues and cells of our body. These energies carry intelligent coding that is evolving every cell of our body to a less dense bioluminous body of light. Human DNA is evolving beyond the typical two strands to a fully activated and revitalized 12-strand system. We are returning to our "Adamic" form, the original divine human blueprint.

Each energy wave brings in new ascension symptoms as the whole human body and consciousness system is upgraded. Every individual is unique in this experience. Many report headaches, cold-like symptoms, hot flashes, ringing in the ears, vivid dreams, burning in the chest, digestive system issues, detoxification symptoms, emotional purging, and more. I talk more about these symptoms and ascension symptom care later in the book.

It should be noted that not all of humanity will be making this transition. These plans were made before incarnating and are not the polarized judgment narrative propagated by world religions. This is part of the Divine Plan, and all souls are playing a part in the great story that is unfolding. Those who will not be transitioning will not be receiving the upgrades to their genetics and will start to deteriorate in health and transition out of the body.

There is nothing "bad" about this. They have simply fulfilled their life plans and will transition out of the body to support the ascension from the spirit side and/or prepare to incarnate again in another form, either on Earth or another planet/realm where they can continue their soul's evolutionary pathway. Physical death is not final. We are immortal beings who have lived many times and will continue to evolve and serve Creation through many more forms in the future.

The Unveiling

Apocalypse is a Greek word meaning "unveiling," "uncovering," or "revelation." This implies that what was once hidden is to be brought into the light of awareness. We see this in the unfolding of events around the world as the unconscious shadow is being brought to the surface to be cleared. In the coming months, we will see more political scandals surfacing and the unveiling of travesties that have been committed over time and kept hidden from the public.

Turn off the Television: Tune into Your Inner Being

Repeatedly in my hypnosis sessions, it has been suggested to turn off the news stations, put down the smartphones, and tune into the presence of Gaia, the Divine Source, and our own Inner Being. The gateway to this new Light Kingdom (Queendom if you prefer) of New Earth is through the electromagnetic field of your own heart and your innate connection to the Grace and Light of Source. Ascension requires us to grow in our capacity to love unconditionally and transform our physical, etheric, and mental bodies through transformative practices and purification. This is what Christ meant when he said to "clean thy robes" to prepare for the next "garment of Light."

This book serves as a guide to illuminate the Ascension pathway and initiate the reader to the Higher Mysteries and Laws of Creation. It aims to explain our origins from the eternal Source and provides a summary of the story of Creation as it relates to cosmic, galactic, planetary, and human history. It gives a futuristic perspective of the revitalized higher dimensional Earth post-Ascension that describes what the New Earth will be like and how humanity will live upon the Earth and with the Star Nations and Hierarchy of Light.

There is a detailed description of the stages of Ascension as it relates to the evolution of the planet, human biology, and human consciousness.

The reader's consciousness is guided into an experiential relationship with their Lightbody, and spiritual energy practices are given to activate, heal, and upgrade the human subtle energy body in preparation for the next "light garment" and higher consciousness reality of 5D New Earth.

TWO

Starseed Phenomenon

Since the fall of Atlantis, many benevolent star beings and high beings of Light have volunteered to come to aid in the freeing of Earth and humanity from endless cycles of suffering created by negative polarity consciousness and karma. All throughout history, there have been secret orders that have carried the pure teachings of Light. These wisdom-carrying communities studied the ancient teachings of science and spirituality passed down from divine prophets and messengers. They mastered the human body on all levels — physical, etheric, emotional, mental, and psychic. These priests, priestesses, sages, shamans, monks, nuns, seers, philosophers, physicians, alchemists, musicians, healers, and scientists protected this knowledge with their lives. They often studied and did their advanced work in secret underground tunnels, remote areas, and cave systems to avoid persecution from controlling powers.

Highly advanced orders such as the Druids, the Essenes, the Melchizedek priesthood, Kabbalists, Rosicrucian, Cathars, Priests and Priestesses of Isis, Indigenous medicine people, master yogis, and so on have carried these teachings throughout time. These wisdom traditions teach of the hidden Mysteries and the secrets of Earth and the Universe. Highly advanced celestial and galactic beings have been incarnating as humans into these communities on the Earth at the darkest times of Earth history to hold the Light and protect the sacred artifacts and teachings so that we do not lose the ancient knowledge from our ancestors and our extraterrestrial and celestial families of Light. Each incarnation, those "on mission" are guided back to the sacred materials to activate DNA coding and remember their higher purpose so that we can continue to support the expansion of consciousness upon the Earth.

With the support of benevolent extraterrestrial beings and the Hierarchy of Light, humanity has been slowly ascending in consciousness. This is still a free-will planet, and direct interference is not permitted. Humanity has to choose peace and unity on our own. Time and time again, humanity has chosen war, domination, and separation. Each moment we have a choice to follow the path of love or the path of fear. That being said, this is the last battle, and the restoration process is underway as many starseeds, and highly evolved souls have incarnated en masse all across the planet at every level of government and cultural influence to deconstruct the shadow structures of the Earth and liberate this world from darkness. It has been said that "It is done." and what we are now watching is the replay of what we have already done and the trickle-down effect from the higher dimensions.

After the Fall of Humanity, the cataclysm of Atlantis, many efforts have been made to resurrect humanity from consciousness decay so that we could remember our divine identity as spiritual beings. We, as individuals and collectively, make our own choices and are responsible for our own destiny pathway. It is not that God has abandoned us; it is that we as humans have abandoned our divine light and have chosen war and destruction repeatedly. The power of our destiny is in our own hands in this free-will universe.

Countless wars have happened all over the planet since The Fall. The teachings of Jesus and the Ministry were distorted and used to torture and kill millions of people for over two thousand years. During the Spanish Inquisition and the Crusades, many people lost their lives "in the name of God," a distorted version of the Divine created by the human ego. Countless libraries of sacred literature were destroyed. During this time, many highly advanced souls incarnated around the world to protect the sacred texts and artifacts left from previous generations that hold keys to our remembrance. Many innocent healers and wisdom keepers were burned, tortured, and slain. All of this happened within our free-will creation. At any point, humanity could have decided to follow a different path.

After two world wars and the development and use of the atomic bomb, Gaia and the spiritual beings who watch over the evolution of Earth and humanity sent out a distress call for help. It was obvious that if something were not done, humanity would destroy itself and the planet. This planet holds vast amounts of significant data stored within its DNA and the Akashic Records (spiritual records). If Earth were to be destroyed, the negative implications would ripple out and affect many other planets and star systems beyond the Earth. A plan was devised to assist Gaia and humanity in their Ascension to avoid the destruction of the planet.

In my sessions, clients describe many ways that the higher realms and benevolent star races developed and activated plans to support Gaia and humanity. Along with Jesus, countless souls volunteered to incarnate as humans to influence Earth from the inside and support humanity and Gaia in this Grand Shift. Dolores Cannon writes about this mission in her book *The Three Waves of Volunteers and the New Earth*, which describes three generations of souls who incarnated to raise the planet's vibration and humanity's consciousness so that we may all ascend.

Common Traits of Volunteers

Volunteers, also called starseeds, blue rays, indigos, and lightworkers, often have a few common traits. Volunteers often feel that they have a big "mission" or something significant to accomplish in their life even if they cannot remember the specifics. They feel a deep connection to the Earth and the natural world. They are disturbed by what is happening to the planet's ecosystems and animal life. Volunteers often prefer isolation over crowds and animal companionship over human friends and feel uninterested in mainstream activities and culture.

Many volunteers report that they feel that they do not "fit in" or they feel "different" than most people, the odd one in the group. This does not mean that they feel "better" than others but feel out of place even with, and often, especially with their family members. It can be quite a lonely experience. Many feel homesick and have spent much of their lives wondering if others have similar "vibes" and perspectives.

Many are highly empathic and intuitive and feel the suffering of the world. Often, they feel abandoned or left on the Earth and want to go "back home" to God or the stars. Many develop heavy addictive patterns to numb the pain of human life and to drown out their hypersensitivity. Some decided to leave early and have committed suicide to exit the Earth realm.

Many souls heard the call to volunteer, and only the best and most suited for the job were selected to incarnate as a human to play out this Grand Mission. Earth life is dense, and nothing can prepare you for all the experiences one can have as a human on Earth. Many volunteers chose to incarnate into the densest and darkest parts of humanity to experience human suffering and transmute it through their light. Even with extensive training and preparations in the spiritual realms and past lives, many were still unprepared for Earth's density and have experienced much suffering at the expense of their service.

Some of the Volunteers have been to Earth before and have traveled great distances to support this global awakening. Most commonly are souls who are starseeds from Sirius, the Pleiades, Orion, Arcturus, and Andromeda. Each of these regions of space has its own planets and schools. To "come" from a certain star lineage means that your soul spent time incarnating and learning in that experimental zone. We all truly come from Source.

The added challenge was that once incarnated, Volunteers would forget where they came from and why they came, but most know that their life has a BIG purpose and may spend a lot of life unsure what that means. While some people have specific directives in their mission and particular things to accomplish, in general, we came here to awaken fully in our consciousness, share unconditional love, and assist in bringing humanity back into union with the Divine and one another. We also assist Gaia in her Ascension by being lightning rods that anchor higher dimensional energy through our bodies and intention.

These brave souls have dedicated their awakened life to "midwifing" this grand birth of higher consciousness. Volunteers agreed to stay relatively unconscious to the mission for some time and begin awakening and remembering the mission at a certain point in their lives. Now, all across the planet, thousands upon thousands of awakened volunteer starseeds are well into their awakening and embodiment process. Many of us have remembered why we are here and are actively working together to raise the Earth's vibration. You will find us teaching classes, performing healings, creating art, writing music, working the Earth, teaching children, and many other activities to raise the vibrations of the planet. Some starseeds have more background roles like bus drivers and janitors/custodians who encounter many people and share their lovelight with all they meet. Many of these jobs are similar to what they have done in other lifetimes, like driving spacecraft or cleaning up experimental zones of space.

Along with the embodied star-seeded volunteers, lightships with higher dimensional beings and extraterrestrial craft are cloaked around the planet, sending powerful waves of energy and love to Earth. They are directing, focusing, and guiding the solar wind radiation from our Sun that carries

DNA upgrades and codes from the Great Central Sun to transform every level of life on the planet. Many star systems and civilizations are involved directly or indirectly with this operation. When the time is right, the disclosure will begin, and humanity will be told about these other advanced beings and their involvement with humanity's evolution. In truth, these beings are other aspects of our Oneself, helping us to remember our Oneness and Divinity.

Many clients are surprised to find that while they have an aspect of their oversoul on Earth (their own incarnation), they have higher dimensional aspects on spaceships and lightcraft outside the Earth's atmosphere. Some even have other aspects of their oversoul incarnated on Earth in different bodies simultaneously, and some even discover that an aspect of them is already in the New Earth reality, preparing to welcome humanity after the shift. We are not just one being. We are One and Many.

This massive multidimensional, intergalactic armada is made of highly skilled and accomplished ascension leaders, master healers, and great cosmic scientists. These beings have achieved high spiritual maturity levels and work together in many star systems to mature consciousness and the various biological experiments throughout Creation. Many of these beings have experienced ascension in multiple lifetimes. They have assisted planetary species by incarnating at key moments to boost consciousness and lead the species through pivotal transformation processes at nexus points in the ascension and descension phases. We move from planet to planet, assisting each realm in its ascension. I once heard an Indigenous elder speak of the changing times and how he was taught by his elders that it is the same souls incarnating again and again to help during grand transitions. In his words, "We have done this before, and we will do it again!"

There are many levels to this process beyond individual ascension. For example, there are spaceships with medical treatment centers to help assist species through transformation. They restore DNA, work with radiation toxicity, clear stagnant emotional energy, and upgrade information stored in the species' consciousness. I have clients describe massive ships, arks, filled with ecosystems teeming with life. Massive holding tanks carry whales that are recalibrated and healed so that they can be readministered to Earth's oceans to energetically clean the waters with their songs. Samples are taken of myriad life forms to be taken to other "Earths" to seed life.

Even physical human beings are being taken onto ships for healing and upgrades, which is especially common for major ascension leaders on the ground. This is not to be confused with abductions and experiments from our past from beings like the "Greys" from the star region of Zeta Reticuli, but friendly interactions with the star family that has been pre-approved from the higher realms before incarnation.

Some ground crew starseeds consciously and unconsciously act as a feedback loop for the Galactic Federation and higher realms. Their bodies subconsciously scan the environment for information which is then sent to ships where information is processed to measure progress and plan for the next steps in assistance. Some starseeds have higher aspects on spacecraft in charge of transmitting positive vibrations to the Earth through advanced crystal technology.

Some starseeds are utilized to activate and restore ancient technology at sacred sites and various points across the planetary grid through their energetic field. Most starseeds can relate to the experience of receiving internal messages or some type of sign to travel to certain places on the Earth or to attend certain events. While they may not seem like anything out of the ordinary, they are guided to move about the Earth to transmute energy, anchor in Light, and meet others on the Mission to exchange coding which is mostly unconscious.

I have had many clients describe being in the higher realms preparing for their next incarnation on Earth. They speak of their excitement to incarnate and bring the power of Love to the Earth. There is much training that happens before they enter their physical Earth life. In fact, many lives are lived in preparation for this Grand Event. Clients speak of higher dimensional training groups where people practice telepathy, telekinesis, and energy healing for when their abilities "turn on" in their physical lives. Everything has been rehearsed so that the proficiency of skill is stored within the subconscious. When the time is right and the veil is lifted, we will have tremendous knowledge and powerful abilities to reform this world into a shining Light Kingdom (Queendom if you prefer).

Some clients describe lives on other planets where the entire species received a telepathic call for help because Earth was in distress. I have had clients describe massive ceremonies where communities celebrated their relatives and comrades who were disembarking to travel across space to help humanity and Earth. Earth has been home to many, many souls over these last 13+ billion years. Countless beings have contributed to this evolutionary garden and to the life force of Gaia. There is much love for Gaia and humanity all across Creation.

Young Masters

The new souls coming into the Earth School are advanced beings of Light here to build a New Earth. These are our future architects, leaders, doctors, healers, engineers, and pioneers of consciousness. They are coming in with higher levels of consciousness and a different perspective of the world. Many do not conform to mainstream society already from a young age. Gender is mutable for many as they are free to explore the full spectrum of gender and sexual fluidity. Many have zero interest in mainstream culture and look at the world in disgust and horror as they watch a seemingly dying world that they will inherit from us.

Encoded in the DNA of our young masters are the star technologies, philosophies, and plans for the building of New Earth. We will teach them to levitate, communicate through telethought, move objects with their mind, and other abilities. They will use advanced quantum physics and the metaphysical arts to build a new civilization of Light. The family structure will change into a more communal support system as humanity reactivates the template of a happy, thriving, diverse village.

It is up to us to forge a future worth living for these young masters. We need to create educational programs and high-frequency environments that guide young people into their mastery and activate their intuitive skills. Meditation practices, guided visualization, and energy healing practices teach them how to self-regulate and tune into their Inner Being. Many of these children have powerful extrasensory perception and vivid dreamtime where higher learning and spiritual communication happen. We need to encourage creativity, imagination, and intuition in these young beings so that they can be the visionaries and revolutionaries that they came to be.

THREE
Starseed Transmissions

This next segment comes from a client named Ariella who had a fascinating regression that I hope to share in full in the future. She was part of a cosmic team of human-like beings from Venus who traveled the cosmos as defenders of Light and Truth. Her team came with Lady Venus and ascended master Sunat Kumara to create a higher dimensional reality upon the Earth called Shambala. This armada of illumined beings brought great love power to the Earth to begin reclaiming the planet from a group they called the "Fallen Ones." The session included several battles between forces of Darkness and forces of Light. At the end of her life, I asked that she be moved to when she was meeting with her guides.

C: *I am reporting to a council of Light...what is happening on Earth and my great concern that there need to be many, many more volunteers to go and help...and to be trained to bring its vibration up...to bring the Love up. And they agree that they will send out a call for that for those who are strong enough to do that. And they said they want me to train those who were going to go down to Earth...to get ready.*

M: **So, tell me what happens next.**

C: *I'm back on my beloved planet Venus and we are training thousands...along with others...I am only one of many. We are training thousands through various initiations and classrooms of highly sacred teachings and abilities. Only those with the most pure intentions can learn how to bend time like I do.*

M: **What kind of training do you put them through?**

C: *The trainings are...they're filled with love, camaraderie, highest respect for each other. It's very, very important that they love others as themselves. They must have a strong connection to Source. This is paramount. They learn the ways of protecting themselves with energy...using energy...the highest vibrational energies...how to stave off and notice when an energy is coming to distort theirs...with this pure shield, with a pure shield. Abilities to see through dimensional walls...see clairvoyantly. Intuitively. Clairaudiently. Being in tune with the person that you are next to. Not taking on their power but knowing their power. Not taking their power or weakness and using it against them, but actually empowering them so they overcome their weakness. It's a very high initiate who is learning these things through the love of others and respect of others and not looking down or overlording or being better.*

It's learning how to teleport...to be able to be anywhere at any time, through thought alone. Through thought. To influence...positively influence...this is a very big one...to positively influence the outcome of the situation through intention and thought. But this must only be for the good of mankind. Not in a negative way. So, also taught: the law of causality and how strict it is...to follow it and see the direct correlation of cause and effect happening simultaneously. It's almost like a martial arts kind of a class, where what you put out is automatically coming back to you. It's very interesting how this particular class is like a mirror game. Whatever energy you are putting out immediately comes back. So, you are seeing everything in the form of that energy and how it materializes very quickly and how it can move against you...and not to use it to move against somebody, so that you are getting immediate effects from good or bad causes. You can see it simultaneously as if it is...as if you are doing martial arts or you are doing swordplay and whatever you have inflicted on anybody else is immediately coming back to you. So that you are learning the law of cause and effect, physically. Very, very acutely. So, it is ingrained in your DNA. So, whatever you are putting out, you are immediately getting the effect. And that you must adhere to this law of the universe. It's very, very paramount. That's one of the classes. It's a very thought-provoking, interesting class to teach the young people.

Transcript: Simulated Training for Earth Mission

Neomi, the client who brought forward the life of Esther, found herself on a monochromatic grey planet. The entire landscape was made of jagged grey rocks and no vegetation. She described her body as grey and blue with the texture of turtle skin. Her home was a simple grey cubicle with a stone bed that she rested on without needing to sleep. Her home had a device that she could insert her head into and be projected into an Earth simulation where she practices being a young human girl playing in a field. When she pulled herself out of the projection device, she looked out of her dwelling to see a large crater where the town was located about seven miles from her home. She followed a jagged path into town and described what she saw there.

C: Then we get into town, and it almost seems like this is training. I feel like I'm in training. So, you go into the town and it's like an older town like in ancient times, like a bazaar. There are wooden carts and people selling things...and like material and food but I know I don't use these things, so this is training. So, I guess if I want to, I can go experience this to learn more. It seems like there are some humans there, but it's an illusion. They're just part of the training.

M: What's the training about?

C: You go to the bazaar, and you interact with the humans, and you can buy things and get food, but we don't eat the food because we don't need it. They have things so you can touch the food. I can pick up an apple and it's super red, but it's not really...this is not an apple like here on Earth. It's like an illusion. It's super bright, neon red. It's like they're trying to recreate it for training, but it's okay. I can hold it. It's smooth. I know that I eat it and that I can look at it and see the stem on it and look underneath and then I hand it back.

M: What's the purpose of this training?

C: So, I can be more comfortable and natural. So, let me walk further into town. So, on the outskirts there are these peddlers I can pretend to buy things from. It's like play. It's like here on Earth I play with my kids, and they make me food with their playset. So, I walk into town and there are little buildings set up, little wooden buildings that you can go into. Very simple. So, there are women wearing long skirts...like Little House on the Prairie. It's like that. So, I went into this building, and it was the general store, and they had all kinds of fun things, candies and such.

Then you go into the next store...and...Oh! It's like a modern-day supermarket! They have all the things, organic stuff, or you can buy the stuff, yucky pesticides...and you have to make a decision of what you are going to buy. So, you have to know to get the organic things, and then there are so many cereals...and not to buy those...and meats and don't buy those. So, there's...it's really hard to buy the food that you need in this store. It's really difficult to look around and find what you should get.

M: A lot to choose from, but nothing you want.

C: Yeah. There are lots of vegetables and fruits you can get organic, but the rest of the store...and people are buying LOTS of things, but they shouldn't be buying that. Hmm...so, that's kind of challenging. Well, I feel like I found... there are nuts, like almonds and cashews on the middle aisle I can eat, and some dried berries and things are okay. And there are the fruits, but I'm trying to find...I can't... there are not very many things in the boxes that I should be...I know I shouldn't be getting those things. So, maybe there is some water, but...let me see... Yeahhh (sighs). There's only one jug of water that is okay to get...so I'll get that.

M: Why aren't there other good waters?

C: There are all these other waters, but they all have things in them you shouldn't get. Oh, gosh! And people are getting them, but they should not...they should not be having that water! There's only the one, these square jugs of water...that are like two...they are bigger than the other gallons of water...and bottles. So, this is really hard because...to pick...to feed yourself...so if you had a family or something it would be hard to feed them...the right things. There are a few choices though, so I think you can make it. So, okay. So that's hard. So let me see what's in the next building.

M: Yeah. Well, you said you were on your way to the crater.

C: Yeah. Well, all this is in the crater. It's a training area. You get to go into these different places, and you know what you should do but then you have to...it gives you an opportunity to challenge yourself and try to make the right decisions.

M: Why are people making the wrong decisions?

C: Because all of it's available...and easy. It's just there so I think they don't know. The other people, they're walking around like zombies. There's no life in their eyes. They're walking around and they're getting these things. They're interacting with each other...but there's a glaze over them.

M: Why do they have this glaze?

C: They can't...there's...they're missing a light. They don't know...they don't know what they should be doing. It's like they're walking around in their sleep. They're sleeping.

M: How come they don't they have their light?

C: I think they just need someone to show them, but no one has touched them yet. I don't know.

M: What do you mean by touch them?

C: If I walk up to this one guy...there's this one guy he's got...he's a middle-aged man in a plaid, blue shirt and he has grey pants on and brown shoes...and he has bright, blue eyes but they're just looking forward, glazed. But I can touch his arm and then he turned and looked at me and he smiled. And now he's okay! Now he sees. Well, that seems so easy...but there are so many people...but I don't know...I don't know if I should touch everybody. But this is training...so...but he came right to life. He just looked at me and he smiled and he... It's like their soul's not...their soul's in there maybe, but it's really trapped. It can't interact.

M: And so, when you touch them, what happens?

C: Their soul came into their body and expanded into their, I'll say, meat suit, and then they're alive. But prior, their meat suit...it felt like their soul was in there, but it was withered...like it was withered inside. If you just touch their arm, then they're okay. They can interact and they have love and emotion, and they look at you. And he is so happy. He's got tears of joy and he's looking at his hands. He's okay. Well, that seems so easy. So, okay.

NEXT SCENE: PREPARING FOR EARTH

C: (There is a light pulsing from over the horizon.) It's sending my...it's sending my fellow beings elsewhere. People are leaving where they stay and so am I. And now we're next! So, I'm supposed to go to beyond the training area in the crater. There's a path that goes beyond there. So, it's kind of a while.

And we're sitting in seats, but we don't have arms on our chairs. It's just a plain, ninety-degree-angle chair carved out of the earthen surface and it's just hard, grey, and they're in lines and we're sitting. So, we're next and I see in front of everyone is...there's a gentleman there and he has a flat circular orb, and it has in it... It's metal on top and bottom and in the middle is this light that's going to pulse...and we're going! So, he's standing there, and he has his hand on the light...it's like a metal, flat lamp and in it is sandwiched the light. He puts his hands on it.

And he's talking to us and he's telling us "Be the love and the light." And he's saying, "Save them and wake them." He's just telling us to go do it. He's just saying, "Save them. Don't let the planet die." He's saying, "Don't let it turn black." He said, "Let it be the Light. It must shine like a star soon. So go and use your training and interact and help them."

And he's saying to just sit back and put our arms by our sides and take a deep breath and he's saying it will not hurt. The light will pulse two times and then you will be there on Earth in your human form. So, we're going to be born.

So, the light... So now I can see myself, the light must be so fast. So, I can see myself being born from my mother. Oh, my gosh! I'm just like coming...I'm just being born, and the nurse picks me up and I'm covered in goo. They cut the cord and I'm screaming. It is so bright, and I'm just being manhandled! All over the place! So, it's not really pleasant. And then my mom left. She went to go have a cigarette (laughter). So...

Then I'm just in this box and I'm thinking it's kind of funny because I just came from like a box, waiting in the side of a mountain, and now I'm in this box! I can't do anything. I'm just waiting for someone to come back. But I'm in a white blanket and I'm cozy and I'm okay, but I really wish someone would just come pick me up and love me, but I'm just separated in this box. They're not doing this right. This is not very loving.

So...my mom just came back, and she smells like cigarettes (laughs loudly). I can't say this to her, but I'm thinking in my brain, "Oh, my gosh! This is going to be quite a ride!" (Laughing) And I feel like I'm really going to have my work cut out for me in this life because this was not in the training, this infant part. But it's okay because I can just get used to this human body because it's really mushy. I'm used to my turtle-like skin. I'm all held together there. This is just...I'm like very floppy. So...I'm...this should be okay because I need to get used to this.

So, I'm okay with the infant stage. So...I didn't think I would have these feelings, but I feel upset, and we'll have to change things from the ground up. So...starting here at birth, this has to change. I feel like I'm being really too picky about the whole thing, but I'm not because I think when I got here, I should have more love. They told us about this interaction and emotions but I'm not getting any. Nobody's doing that to me. I feel like someone should be showing me that and it's not happening, so this should change now...so that's something I'll do.

Transcript: Galactic Council Sends Energy to Earth

I met Manu in Costa Rica through a mutual friend. He had read *The Three Waves of Volunteers and the New Earth* by Dolores Cannon, and we had a lot of fun talking about the material. A few months later, he and I scheduled a time to meet online for a session. Here is a segment from what we discovered!

C: *There's sort of a council of beings. It's sort of a metal floor, metal walls...like a spaceship. And they're small, blue beings. Large circular heads. And bigger soldiers that look kind of like dinosaurs. They're planning some kind of operation. They're sending...they're sending a few beings to Earth. There was a training of some kind. It feels very serious.*

M: What kind of training was this? What was done?

C: It was to blend in. Language. Body language. Tactical movements. Communication.

M: So, they had to practice being human. What else is happening there?

C: There's a window. I see other stars. Some are close by. Suns. White suns.

M: You said there is a mission. What's the mission?

C: Light-encoded DNA filaments. There's an activation process. In the right environment and circumstances, certain beings can unlock certain abilities through light-encoded filaments. We're sending certain technologies through certain beings in order to contribute to this... But the people are not entirely connected with everyone else there. It just feels like they're...they're outsiders a little bit...outside the ship.

M: So, it's almost like they don't fit in, even when they go?

C: Right.

NEXT SCENE: BEAMING ENERGY

C: There's a silver pyramid. There's a bunch of beings in robes standing around it. There's like a ceremony of some kind happening. People are from all different planets now. Different kinds of beings but wearing similar...similar outfits. The top of this pyramid is somehow going to have light emanating from it. It's going to go up off of this planet. There's a real camaraderie among the beings...a collective purpose. There's just compassion and humbleness and a wanting to serve.

Somehow this light is going to help ease the energy...or ease the transition at this time. Seems like the energy is somehow going to go back in time. I think it's something for Earth. Earth is going to go through a portal, but...so it's like...it's going to help with that transition. So, it's sending a certain kind of light resonance. It's going to help raise the collective frequency. Once it reaches that correct time period.

M: So, you're all there together to start this energy?

C: Yeah. There's a representative from each system. Each star system that has intelligent life.

M: What makes Earth so important?

C: Earth...Earth's transition can help trigger the transition of other planetoid beings...can reformat the way the galaxy works. It's a cell in the body of this particular strand of light. If the resonance of that cell is out of correlation with the rest of the cellular structure light strands, it's going to create a dissonant resonance, and having the resonance be harmonic is important for all the frequencies to line up in a row harmonically. It will ripple out. It will affect everything.

NEXT SCENE: ON THE SHIP

C: I'm back and now I'm on a ship. And I'm...this was the original...now. I guess this is the future of where I live.

M: What's happening there?

C: There's an urgency to send a message...to send certain kinds of energy patterns out...which is what we're doing in the physical realm...but a certain frequency alignment that can help with the mission. I guess we're doing our...we're doing a certain part of the larger work on this ship, but we're broadcasting certain light.

M: What's the urgency?

C: It's not a panic...but there's a sense of purpose in terms of accomplishing it in a timely manner. Certain kinds of Light symbols. Certain kinds of symbols that are made of light and energy that can help...if broadcasted properly, can help lubricate. We all communicate telepathically, so we're moving some things around the ship, but mostly we're synthesizing each other. We can connect deeply with each other's minds so it's less about doing, it's more about consciousness.

There is a recommendation to not eat certain foods and to go where there's a lot of stones. The more stones that are nearby, the better...is what they say.

M: So, when they say don't eat certain kinds of food, what kinds of foods are they describing?

C: Like red meats. Things like that. No cream...things that are creamy. No tomatoes. I'm just...things that are red, I guess, aren't healthy right now... Apparently, there's so many species of tomatoes here [Earth]. Many of them were not indigenous to Earth except the small cherry tomatoes. They grew here naturally but the other tomatoes have a high acidic level.

M: Will you be going to Earth?

C: They will send a piece of Light to Earth. They'll imprint the blood of this being with this race. They're going to send these light...these shapes made of light...and they're going to broadcast them at a certain time. And at that time, they'll have a certain kind of imprint...like a sonic imprint on this being so that they can send energy to and from.

M: What's going on with the humans? Why are there so many issues there...that they need so much support?

C: They can't really see what they are and so...like young children, they don't understand what they're becoming. They don't understand the consequences. They don't know how to behave in a way that provides them with access to other frequencies, other experiences, and they need to be looked after the same way that children need to be looked after.

M: Has it always been like this?

C: No. No, no. There are beings that...that like...this particular area of the galaxy would be a good...what you would call "good real estate." So, the purpose is to change the resonance here so that it's not against the rest of the network. If this particular cell can be turned backward in the resonance, then that can spread into other cells. There's a...they've tried to...tried to change the flow in a different direction.

M: Where do these beings come from?

C: Alpha Centauri.

M: And how are they affecting the humans?

C: There's a certain frequency that they send via the Moon and what you would call "cell towers" that can create frequency locks that limit the DNA's lighting code filament and for...they're like consciousness caps. But obviously, there are many here that are not affected by that.

M: What can the humans do to deflect this?

C: It depends on the human. Each one...well...there's a small number that are truly aligned with us, the purpose of moving through Earth's portal, and they are flowing with that energy and are assisting that shift. But the humans at large can all change and grow, wherever they are now, they must evolve...even just a little bit more...grow a little bit more. Develop. Soften. Develop virtue. Center themselves. Every little drop counts. Every little drop matters. There is no waste in this universe.

Open to Your Star Lineages

There has been much fear programmed into human consciousness about extraterrestrial life. Not one of us humans on the planet is "from here." Our species was brought here by extraterrestrials. Our souls come from higher dimensions and have experienced life in many forms and experimental worlds. The negative ET invasion already happened, and they are part of the driving force behind the media and institutions. The craft we see in the sky, disarming military weapons and nuclear power plants and such, are POSITIVE beings here to assist humanity.

We can release our fears and negative stigmas about extraterrestrial life. There are countless species of organic life spread throughout this universe, let alone the other universes and all their experimental zones of creation. There are many intelligent and unity-focused species in our multiverse who are beaming love and encouragement onto the Earth and into the hearts of humanity as we approach our graduation from 3D and move into the multidimensional unity consciousness of 5D and beyond. These are our family members and truly our Oneself in many forms.

FOUR

Making the Transition

This next client, Rachel, was taken to a lifetime where she was working in a greenhouse growing plants to be planted on different planets throughout the cosmos.

C: It's a blue plane, and I can see the surface of the planet, so it is blue, and I can see the curve to the planet. I can see the night sky as the backdrop of the planet. I am just on the planet. There are like craters to it but not so much as the moon. But I can see when I focus that there are structures that fade in and out of existence, so they are not solid. It's like when you put your focus on them, they become a little more solid, but they are not completely solid.

M: That's interesting. What do they look like?

C: Geometric shapes. Like I am getting a rhombus.

M: Very interesting. Is there any plant life or any other life on this planet?

C: No, but I'm getting that if you move into one of these structures, it's a lot more abundant — like plush inside the structures, not on the surface, not that you can see.

M: Well, before we go on that journey, I would like you to look down at the ground and tell me if you can see your feet.

C: It's just a blue energy. It comes more into form as I move up the body so it becomes like you can see in a jellyfish as you move away from the sides. So, in the middle, there's more structure to the body.

M: Are you carrying anything or holding anything.

C: It is like a scepter. It's got a blue beacon — like a round, cylindrical shape on the top, and I think it sends energy. Yeah, it sends energy. It can help the plants grow. So, it revitalizes, and yeah, it expedites their growth.

M: That's nice. Do you have anything else on your body? Any other components?

C: It's like a utility belt. It has seeds in it, different compartments with different seeds.

M: And you plant those around somewhere?

C: In the structures.

M: Well, let's go visit one of those structures. Take me on the journey and tell me what's happening as it happens.

C: So, it has a door that can open, but it's like an energetic see-through door. As you pass through the door and shut the door behind you, everything changes. Like you cannot see the outside. You can't see the planet anywhere once you step in. It's like an atrium of life, of different plant life. There are ferns, and it's mainly green, and it's like the plants are moving on their own — like they can move and communicate with us.

M: That's nice. You said, "us." Are there others like you there?

C: Yeah. In the distance, there are a few others working, tending to the plants. I think I grow them for other planets. So, we cultivate them and grow them, but like they're special in the way that you can plant them on other planets, and they will communicate back to the plants on this planet. And they can talk to these plants and get the information from the planets that we have planted these plants on.

M: So, what do you do with that information once that feedback information has been sent?

C: We collate it and send it up to the motherships and they analyze it. It's to do with the oxygen and the atmosphere of the planet that they get sent to.

M: What about the oxygen? What's so important about the oxygen?

C: It needs to be kept at certain optimal levels.

M: And so, the plants help that happen?

C: Yes. They send the information back up to these plants, and they tell them if more is needed on the planet.

M: Wonderful. That's very valuable information. Do you enjoy your job?

C: Yes, but I want to go where the plants go. I want to visit where they are — to go on adventures.

NEXT SCENE: ON A MOTHERSHIP

C: Now, I am up on the ship. It's like a donut. It's huge. It's like a donut-shaped vessel, and it's got a number of different beings on it from all over the galaxy. There's a lot of humanoid-type beings. Yeah, insectoids — so the mantis beings. Everyone has their own jobs. So, one where I am standing at the moment is the leisure viewing platform. I can see Earth.

M: What's happening on the Earth right now that you all are observing it?

C: The starseeds are bouncing back information about the ascension, the ascension process. They are like beacons of light that beam, then they are collating the information like the most minute detail is recorded and analyzed.

M: And what are you all learning from the starseeds?

C: How to help them balance their own energy. How to help them in their own process. How we put positive intentions down to them without interfering.

M: How do you send the information and help without interfering?

C: Through intentions, our positive and loving intentions.

M: And why is it that you don't interfere?

C: That was a decree.

M: So, there was a decree not to interfere?

C: Yeah. They've got to do it themselves. They can feel us. They can feel us. Yeah. They are connected to us. We are their higher applications.

M: Well, what's happening now? What are you doing?

C: I am just observing people on the observing platform. They are observing themselves. There are people playing music. There are beings specifically there to heighten the vibration to bring joy and love so that everyone on the ship is in the highest vibration possible. So, the serious work it is very joyful and yeah — people — beings connecting with each other and telepathically swapping stories of their journeys. People are talking about the tipping point. It's the buzz in the air about that. They are really excited.

M: What are they saying about the tipping point?

C: That it is so close. People are feeling the energy waves as they are coming in and embracing them and it's making them all over-excited.

M: That's wonderful. What does the tipping point mean to everybody? How do they know they are at the tipping point?

C: Some feel it. It is like an energetic wave of rainbow light that will just be apparent.

NEXT SCENE: BRINGING HUMANS ON THE SHIP

C: We are in the sleeping pods. So, we have our own quarters — our own white rooms that are like large pods that we connect one on one there.

M: What do you mean one on one?

C: Each one of the beings comes in and speaks to each other telepathically, one to one, and shares stories. I am connecting with another being.

M: What are you connecting about? What's being shared?

C: Our lifetimes on other planets. So, this story about children playing on the grass and just being free spirits. And the more that we can share this positive white energy — the more that we can build it and harness it, and then send our intentions to Earth, and help with the energy of pure joy and love.

M: That's so nice. It sounds like you all really love this planet and love your work. Why do you love this planet so much? Why are you so connected to its process?

C: Because part of us is down there. It's an aspect of us on the planet. It is us.

M: What are you seeing happen next?

C: Next, we start bringing people up one by one to acclimate them to the higher frequencies. So, it's only small numbers at the moment that are coming up.

M: How do you bring them up? How is it that you bring them up?

C: I am not sure. I just see them in the pods. They are like jellybean white pods. They spend a few days up in the pod, and we observe them, and some of them come out and join us on the viewing platform, so they understand what's happening to Earth. Some of them didn't understand, so they needed to be brought up and shown.

M: And how do they respond?

C: They think it's amazing. They had a hunch. They kind of knew.

M: Yeah. It's exciting to have the humans starting to come up on the ship. What happens next?

C: They go back and start sharing it energetically. They have this now innate knowing that it is real, and it is happening, and they can share it with others that they have this found faith now that is true. And even if they don't talk about it, they share the vibration with everyone they come in contact with.

M: That's wonderful. What does that do for the people on the planet who might not be aware? How does this vibration help them?

C: It opens their perception — so you see their crown chakra starting to tingle and sparkle when this awareness — the energy touches them. It just opens it up.

M: That's so wonderful. What's happening now?

C: Right now, I have got an overview of the ship, and I am not on the ship anymore. I am sort of floating around it.

M: Do you see any other ships around?

C: I can't see them, but I feel them coming closer. I feel that more of the ships are huge, but they won't take everyone.

M: What do you mean? Tell me about that?

C: Well, at the moment, there are only pods for maybe half a dozen people, but there's much, much more needed. So, I feel the other ships are coming closer.

M: And why are they going to be taking more humans onto the ships?

C: The same purpose. They just have to try it first. They just have to observe what would happen if humans came up and then went back again.

NEXT SCENE: GOLDEN EARTH AND GOLDEN HUMANITY

C: Now there's a cylindrical dome with all these donuts in the sky surrounding the Earth completely. It's like they are all holding energetic hands with each other touching in a circle formation, all the donut-shaped ships.

M: So, they are all surrounding the planet? Why is that?

C: So that all the loving intentions are concentrated on Earth. Well, there's a golden light that's shone upon the Earth...yes, and the Earth is transformed. It's a mixture of all the positive intentions on the ships along with the human intention that kind of join forces, and this golden light just beams from the planet and the planet transforms. It's like the golden light sheds the layer of the outer surface of the Earth and what's inside the Earth comes forward to the new surface. So, the inner Earth becomes the outer Earth. It is like a snake sheds its skin — the inner, renewed part comes to the surface, so it's fresh.

M: That's so nice. Does it change things on the planet? How does it look when it's renewed? How does it...what's the process look like as it happens?

C: Everything looks fresh...the trees are just a new color, like glowing. Everything is more vibrant.

M: That's nice. And what are you doing now? What's happening?

C: I am still observing from afar — the ships and the donut shape and the Earth sort of just coming forth into this new reality. It's quite a sight. It's like you just can't take your eyes off it — so beautiful.

M: I bet. So stunning. What's happening with the people on the planet?

C: It's like the people were just under the surface of the old skin, and they are coming up with the new planet. So, I can see them like rubbing their eyes and seeing the light because they have been down further in some darkness. And they are taking their first breaths and filling their lungs with a new type of oxygen

— like it feels different to them — their lungs. (Takes a deep breath and sighs.) Feels easier to breathe. They have got to relearn a lot of stuff. They have forgotten how to share and how to live in harmony. They've got to relearn communities and to work together — and help one another.

M: How did they relearn?

C: *They just feel it. They feel now that they need to work together. It's just their knowing that they are one, and to help each other benefits all. So, I can see them having different methods now working in fields and with agriculture. They have different technologies to grow, so like the scepter; they use energetic...it's like funneled energy to grow the crops rather than relying on GMO or anything to boost the growth...they can just use pure energy now.*

M: How do they access that energy and use it?

C: *They can bring it up from the center of the Earth, or from Source energy they can channel it down, bring it down through their bodies. Bring down and through their hearts, or they can use tools...there are scepters that are receptors.*

M: And where do they get these scepters from?

C: *There are now visitors from off-planet that are welcome.*

M: So now the space families are now coming back onto the planet?

C: *Yeah. There's no fear anymore. The humans don't perceive as they used to. It diminished. It dissolved with their renewal.*

M: Wonderful. Has anything happened to the human body now that the shift has happened?

C: *They can absorb more light and they breathe in the oxygen. It is a lot freer. So, when they breathe in more light, it just fills them up so more efficiently with light than it ever has before. So, you don't need to concentrate on filling yourself up with light anymore. It just happens automatically with each breath. So, the energetic body is renewed with the light, and each cell is a lot more light-filled. The humans can choose whether they want to be in their solid form or move into the golden light form.*

M: Tell me about those two forms.

C: *So, the human form's a lot like we have now, but just more golden and light-filled, but they can with intention completely move into this golden light form. It allows them to move to different planets...they can move wherever they want. They can move to the other side of the planet.*

M: Wonderful. So, they just shift into this golden light form and just travel?

C: It takes a lot of practice. It doesn't happen straight away but the ones that are already on their ascension path, they can master it a lot more quickly because it is like when you meditate and you go out of the body — it's that feeling; that feeling signature that you lose, you lose contact with your body. The body dissolves and moves into this golden-white form and then you can reanimate however you choose.

M: Wonderful. So, when humans travel off the planet or around the planet, what do they do when they are doing this traveling?

C: So, it depends on what their interests are. So, for example, the planet that I was first on and was shown — they will go to those planets to learn agriculture and learn the new ways of doing things and take it back and apply it there.

M: That's wonderful. What do you see happening now?

C: I see the Earth is less densely populated because of this. So, because they can move freely once they have mastered the movement and it becomes much less densely populated, which gives space for new growth and for the Earth to really regenerate itself to its former glory — to its heaven on Earth. She becomes the true oasis.

M: That's wonderful. So, it just starts to get regenerated because fewer people are there, more information is coming in, more knowledge?

C: Yeah. It's like self-perpetuation, regeneration. It's been slow going to begin with — like it's still happening now. It is very dense and slow, but once this intentional shift from the star beings and the healings — once that is a collective concentration, it happens more quickly.

NEXT SCENE: GREAT CENTRAL SUN RAINBOW BRIDGE

C: It's like a pure, rainbow-white-stream column coming down to Earth. It's like a waterfall column that's going straight into the Earth.

M: Where's it coming from?

C: The Great Central Sun.

M: And what is this light doing? What is this rainbow light stream doing?

C: It's bringing in the even higher density energies that have never been possible before, like six density, twelve density — like a huge portal. The Earth couldn't sustain those higher energies before.

M: What are these energies doing?

C: I am not sure. I am just watching the energy go back and forth. It's like a stream.

M: It sounds very beautiful.

C: Yeah, it's directly from Source. Before it's been filtered, and it couldn't come so seamlessly through. I am not sure of the higher purpose of it.

Transcript: The Rainbow Bridge

Another client shares a bit more about the "rainbow bridge" concept.

M: Why is it important to keep singing?

C: The powers that are trying to repress the people do not want you making sounds, noise. They know... They don't want you gathering to sing together. After three minutes of singing together, everyone's heartbeat syncs up to the same rhythm. They don't want us synced up. What they are trying to block ultimately is the ascension, and so when you sing together it helps the group ascend together.

We are all going on a journey together; we're walking each other home. We're climbing a giant mountain and it's a long steep path. You can only go one at a time on this journey but when you look in front of you there is a line of people in front of you, and when you look behind you there is a line of people behind you, and the people in front of you are not better than you, the people behind you are not below you, they're just two minutes...it's just a timing thing. They're just two minutes behind you on the road. It's not a good, better, or worse but we're all going together.

Where we go one, we're all going, and we have to go together (crying). It's sad to see the fear and to know that...even as I stand on the trail, I see those standing in the woods that need to get on the trail and they're afraid, but we're not...like nobody gets left behind.

M: What does that mean, "No one gets left behind?"

C: It means that this will take as long as it takes until everyone that got promised ascension to, at this time the promise was made, and so the population on this planet is very specific to the ascension. People who tell you that the planet is overpopulated don't understand the spiritual significance of what's going on right now.

We're not having this giant population to like damage and rape the Earth or anything like that. It's to do...it was to bring down as many experts...like all the ascension experts are here now, in body, whether they know it or not, they're the ascension experts and they're all down here now to get us to twenty...you know, to get us through the next two decades as we work through this process. I don't know the timelines specifically of how long it's going to take, but I know it takes to get everyone across the rainbow bridge, to get everybody over the bridge, to get everybody up to the peak.

FIVE

Main Wave Event

This client came to see me to facilitate a surrogate session for her husband who has had difficulty accessing the information he wanted in previous sessions. One of the ways I do surrogate work is first to do a full IQH session for the new client and then ask if it is appropriate to receive healing and information for the person requesting the surrogate session. This works best when the people know one another but it is not necessary. All is connected through the unified field of Consciousness.

The surrogate client is named Mona who did a session for her husband Ian. In the session, her Higher Self uses the analogy of "clean air" which symbolized "clean emotional and psychic energy" earlier in the session. Although, I have a feeling this could also mean literal clean air as major smoke and pollution have been talked about in other clients' sessions. The time period given for this energy event pulse is estimated around 2024.

M: Question about, she does not feel the urge or the excitement to travel. Is there anything behind that?

C: *Something is coming, a strong wave of energy. It's coming. And when it comes the house will fall. It will shatter everything they believe in. Their family will need their guidance then, so they cannot be absent. That is why they can't leave, not now. They need to be present for this wave, so they can lead the house into the new phase. It's going to be a new movement. The air will be clear then. Once it's clear, their lungs will not know how to breathe in the clean air. They have been plagued with. The family will need them then. They'll need guidance.*

M: What is causing this wave? Where is it coming from?

C: *It is coming from all around the Earth. It is going to push out all bad energy. It will be extraordinary. The movement will cleanse everything. And those who have lived in darkness will not know how to breathe in the clean air. They may not be able to adapt. Ian does not want to leave them behind in the darkness. Neither does Mona. That's why they don't want to leave. They want to guide them, The people they love, they want to guide them into the light when this happens. So that they're not left behind. Their hearts have a strong light, but their lungs are full of dark energy that they have been breathing in collectively.*

Mona and Ian have been adapting. They have been cycling through this dark air, through their lungs, and cleansing it with the clear air that they have created in their space. They know how to remove it from their systems and how to accept the light. They need to lead both their families. They need to teach them how to adapt to what's coming.

M: When you say it's coming, how, how soon? You can use Mona's understanding of time.

C: There's vibration in her hands now. It's very strong. She senses it's close. The vibration is very strong in her hands. She could sense that it is very, very close. It will be in your lifetime. You will experience this on Earth. It's coming within the next few years. Before they leave this home, they will experience this new Earth. It's coming. It will be two years. That's when the wave will come. It's already started to build up.

M: What will it be like here on Earth From now until then? What's this time about? Globally? Personally?

C: There will be great darkness that spreads around the Earth, leaking into everyone's lungs. Trying to stop them from being able to adapt to the light that will come. As it will be very heavy. Will fall into a depression. And all of the senses; financial, emotional, mental, everything. They'll fall into a dark depression and their lungs will be filled with darkness. They will need to remember how to breathe in the light. Only those will be able to pass through the new wave. They need to remember that after the darkness comes the light. They need to be patient and not forget what they are. What they can be and the light inside them. They can overcome the darkness that will come to pass. There will be light on the other side and fresh air to fill their lungs. All the darkness will disappear if they just learn how to breathe it in and accept it in their heart.

M: Is there any other guidance about this passage between now and the big wave of light?

C: The vibration will cause pain. It will cause physical pains. It will lead them to believe their health is deteriorating but it isn't. This is only the body's adjustment to the new wave, the new vibration of the new Earth. Once the wave comes the pain will subside. They need only to endure. It has been coming for the past few years. That's why all this pain is arising. All these strong emotions are arising. It's heightened now. We're at the peak. You need only endure this time as you have been enduring in past years. It's slowly been building your strength. That we are at the peak. You need to build your strength further so that you can endure what is to come. If you endure it, you will be ready to accept what's happening on the other side of the wave.

M: What about planetary changes? Earth changes? Do those begin before or after the wave?

C: There will be drastic changes after the wave. I cannot share them now. They will be severe. New Earth cannot survive as we are now. These changes must occur. There's no need to be afraid. I feel that many fear this new Earth. There's no need to be afraid. We all need to endure these two years. Everything will be okay.

M: And how can people endure this? Or assist others in enduring?

C: Do not give in to the darkness that will fill your lungs. It will come from all directions. To make you believe that humanity is hopeless, but it is not. This is only an illusion. It is only an illusion to fool you all into believing that there is only darkness but there is light. You just need to keep the hope. Keep believing in the light for it will come to those who are patient. Those whose hearts are strong. Those whose hearts are strong need to lead those who are weak. Lead them out of the depression, out of the darkness. You need to share what little light we have. Shine it on those who are drowning in the darkness. That is their role. That is our role.

M: Yeah, thank you. I know for many that there are concerns about... I'm going to be careful with my words, um the things that were injected, put into people's arms over this last time. And how it might negatively affect people or the process of this awakening. Can you share anything about that?

C: It will make their process more difficult. The thing they injected is part of the darkness. It's part of the larger cloud that has trickled down. It has been put into millions of people. This will make their process more difficult. It will make it much harder for them to remove the darkness in their lungs because now it is in their bloodstream as well. It was part of a ploy to pull mankind darker and deeper into despair. It will cause many health problems. It will make it feel like there is no hope. They had to endure only a small amount of pain. Now, those who accepted this into their bloodstream will endure severe pain. Their journey will not be easy. They have been fooled by the darkness into accepting this into their bloodstream. but it's not hopeless. They can persevere.

M: How can they persevere? How can they be supported?

C: They need leaders. They need to be led by those who can breathe the light. Mona feels a great sense of responsibility. Her body is being crushed by the weight. She knows she's one of the leaders. Her body is not ready to accept this fate yet. It is creating a crushing weight, vibrations in her body are shaking her very core. She needs time to accept this fate. She will be ready but not now. This realization is causing the vibrations to intensify in the palm of her hands and her knees. She needs time to accept her destiny, but she will be ready. All those who are meant to lead will be ready when the time comes. No need to fret. We will not put any weight upon you that you cannot do.

M: Very good. Thank you so much for that. I had one more question about this wave of light when it comes through. When it moves through, how will it change our experience of reality?

C: The waves will push what humans call "the soul" out of the body and the physical and the spiritual bodies will become separated. Once it's pushed out of the physical body, the cleansing would happen. The spirit [subtle bodies], as they call it, will be cleansed from the darkness but those who keep the darkness within them will stay tethered to the physical body, and they will not be able to be separated.

You will still be able to communicate with those who are still tethered to the physical. But the chances to guide them to the light will be few. The chances to guide them will be much more difficult. There will be few if not none. The guidance should happen before the wave. This is very, very important. Those with the light need not doubt themselves. They need to rebel against the ideologies of humanity. They need not worry even if they're not accepted. No harm will befall them. They need only spread the light and those who will accept will accept and those who will not will also continue on their journey, but no harm will befall the leaders, the spreaders of light. They need to start acting. The time is now.

M: So, question regarding, so it sounds like this soul or this spiritual energy will separate from the physical body for those that are making this transformation but they'll still be able to interact with the people in the physical body that didn't make the transition?

C: Yes. The people in the physical body will doubt the movement. They will not believe that it has occurred. They will see those who are on a higher vibration as though they are their old selves, but they will not be so. Their eyes will view them as they always had but those who are on a higher vibration will know the difference between the two. Doubt will blind them from what has happened. People in the physical body will blind themselves with doubt. They will make themselves believe that the movement was not real. So, when we try to guide them through the spiritual body the doubt will greatly tether them down to the Earth and the physical world. It will be very hard to guide them once you are on a different plane.

M: And those that are in the physical bodies what will they be experiencing, sensing once the shift has happened?

C: *They will feel nothing. They will live senseless lives continuing on and feel nothing. No happiness, no sadness, no purpose, no fulfillment. It will continue on like robots completing daily tasks that have no meaning and no purpose. But they will not understand this. They will only continue on this path until the time when on this Earth has ceased. After that beings that are physical will no longer be created. The entire Earth will shift to a new vibration once all the physical bodies have deceased and moved on.*

M: *Those that have made the shift in, let's say to the New Earth energy, when the wave comes through will they be on a different planet, will they be in a different plane, will they be seeing everything and just standing right next to those people who are still in the darkness? How does that experience happen?*

C: *The Earth will change. They will still be here, but they will be able to travel and experience the Earth in very different ways. They can travel in the blink of an eye to wherever their hearts desire. They will not experience the Earth the same as they did in their physical bodies. Nothing will be the same as they know, everything will be new and beautiful. They may still communicate with the physical humans, but this is only to ease the separation of the connections they have created while they were here. That is its only purpose. To ease whatever regrets they might hold with this separation, to not pull them back down into the physical world. To reconnect with those they have loved. The only reason they can connect and speak with those who are in the physical bodies. So that they can be free of it, free of doubt, and free of the question 'what if?'*

M: Can you give an example of what the ones that shifted to the new Earth, let's say, within the... once it shifts what are the activities that they'll be involved in right after that shift has happened? For the next days and weeks after that wave has come through.

C: *In the beginning, there will be a very slow shift. They will, it will allow time for them to shift their minds from the physical to the next plane. To shift their hearts from what they loved here and to understand that it's okay to move into the next plane. That is why we allow their connection, and communication into the physical world. So that this shift will become easy. Once they have completed this phase.*

M: That makes sense.

C: Once they have completed this phase, they will leave the Earth. Into the abyss of the universe. And then they will know their real purpose. I cannot share more than this.

M: When you say they will go into the abyss, these are the ones that have shifted? The ones that have ascended.

C: Yes. Once they have detached all of their connections from the physical world then, and only then, will they be able to move to the next plane.

M: Okay. I understand that. And you were saying the ones that were stuck in the darkness, stuck in the physical, like they stayed there and that there would be a point where they wouldn't be able to make new life, new children coming in...will there be great deaths that happened rapidly?

C: They will not seek to reproduce. The emotions that they have now, that lead their lives, will no longer plague them. They will only continue on until they decease.

M: And that decease will it still happen gradually over time, or will there be other experiences that create more rapid exits?

C: Many people will pass on, as they say, quickly after the wave, They will accept that they did not move on to the next phase and they will pass on. Many people have already passed on and have started to do so. But there will be a rapid amount of death after the wave. But some people will hold on much longer and will take much longer to accept that it is time for them to move. They will grow to old age and then die naturally. Because of the doubt of the movement that is blocking them from believing.

Transcript: Restoring Earth with the Children

I had the pleasure of working with this client, Dina, around five times including the one where the story of Jeremiah, a disciple of Jesus, was brought forward. In many of her lifetimes, she was a protector of a holy blue flame that emanated evolutionary higher consciousness coding to the Earth plane. The theme of the "blue flame" has come up in several sessions with clients in different time periods. It seems to play a big part in the balance and harmonic evolution of the Earth.

C: *Rolling hills. A river. And a large, very white light pouring out of me. Hands on the ground. It's like my shape is shifting between human form and something not so human. Angelic light being. There's blue light flowing into the ground and connecting different energetic points in the ground. My hands are really hot.*

It's helping fortify and raise the vibration of Mother...of giving the Earth the power to shift on a cosmic level. This shift will cause huge vibrations on Earth's surfaces. Volcanic eruptions and earthquakes...large waves. It's like resetting the clock. There are many of us all over, not just where I am, but all over the planet. It's like every corner of this grid has a key that needs to be placed in it and turned so that the door can open, so the Light can shine through. I guess in a visual sense, if you can picture the chakras of a human body and each chakra...as you open it, it needs a key to be twisted in a clockwise rotation to make the vortex of the chakra start spinning faster and faster.

M: **And so, when you lay your hands on the ground, how does the key work?**

C: *At first, it's pouring energy in, and then it's finding the electromagnetic fields, pulling and spinning it out with one hand on the Earth and the other moving in a clockwise position outward and then upwards, towards the sky. It's like just as bodies have to unwind, so does this grid. We're continuing the work of creating one river and merging all the bodies of water energetically to flow as one. This takes many people. It's like...the four elemental bodies: fire, earth, water, and air will be coming back to their purity, merging as one, and we as lightworkers, we as healers of humans and of Earth will be connecting these bodies of water, these energetic bodies of water together again to purify. It's like cleaning the water. Making it drinkable again. It's like the water is changing from a muddy color to a blue jade, clear water all the way down to the bottom. The trees and the leaves and nature are so green. It's overgrowing. Some of the cities...so fresh and vibrant. It's like the leaves are singing.*

M: **So, everything is being restored. What else is happening?**

C: *A much simpler lifestyle. People are dancing and singing. We see lots of children's faces as they laugh. And the children are huge helpers in this process as they are showing us...what true joy there is in our childlike nature. Helping us hear the plants talk and which rocks need to be collected from the rivers to be placed into other rivers. Some of the elders know, but really the children are the ones that are tasked with going and picking the rocks.*

M: What's so unique about the rocks that they need to be moved from one river to another?

C: The rocks are the densest form of energy. Slowest moving. Longest to change over time. So as these rocks are placed in rivers, these old energies can move in with the moving water and flow and spread downstream. It's learning how to combine light energy with the denseness of the Earth and converting the denseness into light.

WORKING WITH THE HIGHER SELF AND THOTH

M: What about the restoration of Gaia?

Thoth: *Most will see it as the world on fire, but it is from the ashes that the beginning will rise. It is from the dust that we will form a new earth. Pure waters will flow, and waves will crash down, and Mother will shudder and shake, and new life will come from it. As the restoration comes forth and unfolds, you pillars of Light need to stand strong, expand your arms, share the message, and the love. So much love is needed.*

M: What about the human changes?

Thoth: *It's a slow progression. Many years until humans are shapeshifting back and forth between angelic bodies and human bodies, which is why the groundwork is so important right now...in order to prepare the vessel for the energy coming out of your hands...may not be blue yet, but the light will come soon.*

Like a Thief in the Night

In the Bible, it is written that no one knows the hour or the day of when this shift will occur and that it will come as a "thief in the night" surprising many with a quickening of energy and a PULSE of LIGHT. Projected dates come and go which take all who are focused on them on an emotional roller coaster ride. To avoid unnecessary suffering, it has been recommended to stay present in the NOW and allow the process to unfold. Surrender to the process and align yourself with joy and peace as you walk your path towards the New Earth!

SIX

City of Light

This client came to me with some questions regarding her dreams where she was astral traveling to training courses to prepare herself for the shift. She also frequently visited an astral healing center that she felt would eventually be on the Earth. Her inner messaging said that she was going to play a part in that sanctuary space and that it would be in her hometown area in the Pacific Northwest.

C: *I'm talking to Spirit. Or something.*

M: **About what?**

C: *I'm not done. I'm not done with what I was doing to help. Going back, going down on Earth. To be human, I think. To help. I'm excited. I know I can help people. I know I can wake them up. I have to wake myself up because I have to forget. When I wake up, others wake up.*

Going to be in the United States. It's very important to be in the United States. They need help. There's help all over the world. The United States needs a lot of help. I'm going over. I can see cities. I can see cars. Roads. The West Coast is very important. Bringing light like a beacon.

M: **What are some of the plans for that life?**

C: *To heal. To bring awareness. Bring spirit. Can make people's focus shift. They're not focused on anything. There are a lot of distractions that need to be simplified. People's work needs to be simplified. Their thoughts need to be simplified. The way they live. There needs to be more spirit. More light. I keep seeing the Northwest.*

M: **Let's focus there, what's important in the Northwest?**

C: *Something starts there. I feel like it starts I chose to be in the Northwest because it starts in the Northwest.*

M: **What starts there?**

C: *The shift. People want more peace in their lives. They want to be less stressed. They start wanting to be at peace. (**M: Yeah.**) I feel a lot of energy. There's going to be a lot of energy.*

M: **What's going to bring that energy.**

C: *I think it's the center. Like a star. A light. Shimmery. That's where it's coming from. It pulses kind of, but there are different energies. The star is familiar. I feel like I've seen it before. The energies cause things to happen, causes people to think differently. I'm questioning a lot of things. It feels like there's going to be movement, but I don't know. I feel like people are going to start grouping together. They're going to start reaching out more. They want to know what's happening. A lot of chaos there too. A lot of people look confused and think it's scary. Very chaotic. Panic. Fear. I feel like there is some natural... There's something natural happening too, with the weather. The weather is scaring people. They're scared by what it's doing. I feel like there are storms. A lot of water. Rain. People driving. They want to leave, and they want to leave quickly. They're scared. I feel like areas are going to flood. There's going to be flooding. A lot of rain. Wind. Cold. People are getting angry with each other. The ones who are scared are getting angry with each other. They're snapping at each other a lot. Nobody knows what to do. Nobody knows where to go, but they can't stay. Not there.*

M: Where do people go to be safe there?

C: I feel like they're driving away from the cities. A lot of people are going into the trees. There's something there that can help them. Like they feel safe in the trees, but they don't know why they're going to the trees. I feel like some are being drawn to the trees; they feel drawn to the trees, some feel like they're trying to hide.

M: When you said people were starting to get together, where are people getting together there?

C: I feel like there are groups that start before the chaos starts, before things get really chaotic. Before the weather does that. I feel like they group together. They start asking questions and understanding, kind of, that things are changing. I feel like they group together in the trees, and they help each other. Like they're starting a community. Some people get there, and they're scared, and they're confused. Some people look very comfortable and they're helping the ones who look confused. There is a machine that they put people into. They can put people into. It looks like energy. Energetic, healing. It's a white machine. You lay down and something arcs above your body. It feels like it heals you, helps heal you.

M: Where did they get this machine?

C: I feel like the blue people gave it to them. People are healing. Some people are sitting down. There's a man crying. Very scared and he's confused. There's something that's happened. Looks like something major has happened with the world. A lot of weather. It seems bad to people, but it's not really. Very soon.

It looks like there are people who heal the ones who are distraught, and when they're healed, you can physically see light from their hands to the people's hearts. Their foreheads. Their hands are directly on them. I still see the light.

M: So, they're healing them with light? Hands-on healing?

C: Some people are being sent off. There's a woman there. I don't know her nationality. She kind of seems to be in charge a little bit.

M: What's her name?

C: I don't know her name. I don't feel like I know her, but she's expecting people. A lot more people. Healers who can heal people. Then there are people who she's talking to, and they walk away like she sent them somewhere. Maybe to help bring more people.

M: How are people brought?

C: I see people walking into a clearing. They're coming through the trees. Some trickle in, just a few, and sometimes there's a lot more people that come in crowds and when the crowds come, the healers move very quickly. Very swiftly. People when they're healed, they want to know what's happening. And you tell them it's not for them to worry about right now but to just feel the way they feel because when you heal them, they feel better.

M: How did the healers get this ability to heal so rapidly?

C: I think the machine does something. The machine looks like it goes through the pores; it goes through the bodies. Everything. It looks like a lot of them did work on their own too.

M: What's happening now?

C: Some people are sitting underneath the trees. It's very pretty, very pretty where we are. It's easy to forget about what's going on out there. People are still in states of distress. People, healers it looks like, are running out. They move very smoothly. Something about the way they hold themselves that's different. They hold themselves very confidently, very peacefully. Very fluid. Their motions are very fluid. And they go straight up to people, and they'll kneel and they place their hands on them. Seems like on the forehead and the heart. Seems to be the main ones. And we put our attention for healing and peace. You can tell that they feel it when it's happening. When they're being healed, they can feel it. I think it surprises some people. They didn't realize they were in pain.

M: What do they call this place?

C: I want to say Eden, but that was my feeling. It feels like an Eden. Very peaceful.

M: I wonder if you can find the leaders of this place?

C: I feel like some have communication with the blue people. I feel like some have better telepathy. Some can communicate with them. Others I don't think are too interested. They leave it up to the others who can. I see some who've been healed, maybe this is later, some who have been healed. And they're playing with each other in the trees. It looks like we stayed, but where does everybody sleep? I don't know. It feels like we've stayed though. I see people talking. It seems like there are more people.

M: More people that are coming?

C: More people that are already there now. That's why it feels like we stayed. (M: Yeah.) Some feel or look like they're feeling lighter, but there's still self-work, I think. They're still healing.

M: What ways do they heal themselves?

C: They play and talk to each other. There are arguments at times. When they argue, there are groups, there are groups that help them like talk about what came up with them to cause an argument. What were they holding on to?

M: You said there are groups that are doing this work together?

C: Yeah. There's talking. When there is an interaction with someone that's not good, they work through it right there.

Transcript: Building New Earth Temples

David was introduced to me by another friend at brunch when David was traveling through our town from Egypt. I shared about my work, and he immediately wanted to have a session. During his session, we met his Andromedan soul aspect and found out more about the City of Light in the Pacific Northwest.

C: A star being on a golden throne. Looking at the Earth and emanating Light, like a ray.

M: What does this ray do?

C: Activate and heal.

M: What do you call yourself? What do they call you there?

C: Arius. I'm approaching the Earth. My ship is like a golden eagle. As it enters the atmosphere, it becomes transparent. I become transparent. I go down and meet my allies. We hug and greet and celebrate the joyful union.

M: Are these human allies?

C: They're mixed beings. They appear human; they're not. There is something supernatural about them and royal. They're telepathic and their eyes are glowing. There is so much love, and we're holding each other and creating this grid. Building a grid of Light that protects this planet, cities of Light, temples, pyramids, crystal altars.

It's the art that we're trained to do. Build civilizations and train them and hold grids of Light built on free energy and resonating with star frequencies and creating a unity of what is above below. It becomes a sacred mirror and miniature cosmos on the planet basically. It reflects the microcosm. The structures are harmonic, and they have the sacred ratios and geometries and material that we use that can help hold those frequencies.

M: Who trained you to do this?

C: The Creator. It's part of my lineage. It's just our art. It's our gift. I've studied it; it's in my DNA. My DNA trained me.

M: Why are you doing this on the planet now? On the Earth?

C: Because there has been a lot of destruction and we are building harmonics, and the Earth is ascending. New life emerging, like springtime. All the timelines and the multidimensional aspects of myself are coming together. Celebrating this moment and the union. Feeling accomplished, the big job on the higher planes and watching it manifest on the earthly planes. So much heart.

M: Who else is involved in this building?

C: Elohim. They are igniting the sacred fire that powers the grid.

M: Beautiful. Tell me what's happening now. What do you see here?

C: Sacred fire surrounding the Earth, spreading crystal light flames. Transmuting negativity. Shifting the tones, the frequency of the planet. More crystalline structures are emerging from the surface, from the Inner Earth out, and more of the mythical beings coming back to the surface. The children are really happy, and they're playing. Their parents look very much awakened. It is like our Elven DNA is coming back into full operation.

It's the closing of a cycle. Our job is done. It's time to move onto other planets and see them. And so, we say goodbye (deep exhale) and leave.

WORKING WITH THE HIGHER SELF

M: Can you share more with us about his mission? What is he here to do?

C: Build new Cities of Light.

M: Can you share with us that process? What is it like? What will he do?

C: Yes, it starts with one phase, one healing center, one temple. He'll create a template, and he'll go with a team to replicate, recreate according to the energetic structures of the land, and adapt to them. It will be places of high frequencies that attract people to come and thrive and create and move from one spot to the next and rebuild these temples with these templates.

M: Where is this first temple space?

C: Here [Ashland, OR]. It's near some water and forest and mountains. It's very sacred, mystical.

M: Beautiful. Is there anything else that wants to be shared about that center?

C: It's a sun gate. It's a gate to the Sun. A gate to Source. A higher dimensional portal grounded in the physical where the magic happens.

Sanctuary Communities

There will be multiple "Cities of Light," multiple sanctuary communities around the Earth. Everything will align for these communities to manifest in accordance with the Divine Plan. Let us continue our inner work and work within our local communities to raise the collective vibration. Let us follow our inner guidance to lead us swiftly and easily towards our Higher Destiny.

SEVEN

After the Shift

A lina came into her first scene and described a big theater room that was being used for a council meeting. There were many important people gathered to hear her give a report. Some were human and some were non-humanoid intelligent beings. When she looked down at her body, she described it as her body but upgraded and enhanced. Everyone is in celebration mode and is excited to hear what she says in her mission report.

C: Mission completed!

M: What were you completing?

C: Good question, good question. Transportation has been completed with great success. They are in remission, and everything went according to plan, but then again, we knew this wouldn't be easy. So, me and my crew are the ones that have been working with this and seriously need some healing and R&R. [rest and relaxation] (laughs). But we are all very happy that this work has been done. I have a feeling that this was transporting the, shall we say, lower frequency souls off from Earth into quarantine or wherever. Different locations for different categories, but we've moved the ones that needed to go first. Yeah. Some were resisting, of course, but they all went in the end.

M: Where did you send them to?

C: Colonies, but they were in different locations. Some back to Source, some to colonies, some to healing chambers of some sort...rehabilitation of some sort.

M: What is being shared by the group now? How do they handle it?

C: They are relieved and happy, and the feeling is, "We knew we would do this, but thank god it's done." (Laughs). Though it's not complete, this part is completed.

M: Are there other parts that you know about?

C: Similar, but these were the lowest-frequency entities. So, we took the toughest, roughest, first — the worst, if you will, first. Yeah, because they now have to go through the cycle of, shall we call it, karma — cause and effect of what they chose to experience in this experiment. And we are grateful that they did because we needed them to do that for us, but as we are now shifting, they were given the option to shift but chose not to. So, these are the ones that chose not to shift. They have now been relocated.

M: What was the process of relocating them? How did you take them?

C: They were grouped. So basically, I, the people on the ground did that and I was steering the fleets. I was in command of all the ships and fleets and making sure that everyone got on the right ship, that everyone was there basically. But I was in the highest command of this, so I had my crew, or people, report to me. But I am very hands-on, so I am always there also with everyone. We are doing this together.

M: Was this obvious to the humans on Earth? Did they feel it?

C: No, not to all, no.

M: How was it taken without people noticing?

C: I can't speak to that.

M: What's happening now?

C: We are discussing more about everything. Everyone in the room knew the plan, and so we're just going through and confirming what happened and what we did was successful in the end. Yeah, just basically going through it. Some are asking some questions about the details, but that's not important. Everyone is really focused and happy and relieved because this was a huge task, and it was important that we get it done in time. We were on a very tight schedule, apparently.

M: What made it so tight?

C: We were standing by to execute when the command came, and when it came, it had to be done right away; the timing was very precise from Source or whomever. So, when we got the command, it was go, go, go, go, go! We were able to beautifully coordinate, so really, it went smoothly for that type of job.

M: Very good, what will the council do now?

C: Celebrate.

NEXT SCENE: WHERE SHE LIVES IN THAT LIFE

C: Oh, it's down here. It's here, literally here [current house], but I have other places as well. I travel a lot. I have many bases. I go everywhere. Ships, other planets, different places on Earth, different star systems, different galaxies.

M: What do you do when you're in these places?

C: Work (laughs).

M: Tell me about your work. See yourself doing it and tell me about it.

C: I am laughing because I get paid to talk. I am organizing; I am structuring; I am commanding — not from the human perspective of commanding — delegating maybe is a better word. I am, shall we say, the spider in the web connecting all the different works being done and going wherever needed in any given now moment to assist in any operation...in any specific location. And then I go, and I report back to this room. I have different briefings as well, of course.

NEXT SCENE: FLYING AROUND THE WORLD

C: I am flying.

M: What are you flying through?

C: Good question. I am in my body, so I am flying down here on Earth. I am not really doing anything, just flying. I am pretty high up, so I am sort of in the clouds. I don't really see much. I think I am flying over the ocean. I think I am crossing the Atlantic. I feel like I am going back to New York, or something like that. It looks like the streets of New York.

M: What do you notice about the streets of New York?

C: I'd say they're glowing a bit more than I would imagine they are not, but I feel it looks pretty similar. I haven't actually been so...

M: So, what are you doing visiting the city?

C: Yeah, I think it's like a business trip. I'm really all about business, aren't I? (Laughs) It's consulting. It's the same. I am doing consulting in anything, everything, new versus old. Transitioning. I guess I am going into another type of those meetings that we were just in.

It's the same thing as before in how things work. Ah, this is the transition work. These are very sensitive times because we are reshuffling so much. People are going to be shifting out of their old roles; the ones who aren't already in the positions of their passion are going to leave, and they will be redirected by their higher aspects to their proper positions. But this transition is, of course, sensitive from the human perspective because many people are going to be leaving and starting new. And so, there are a lot of fears involved in this, though everyone is handling it without...it's just sensitive. We need to have compassion for everyone doing this transition because even though they are mentally aware that they are going somewhere better, it's still an experience for them to make this transition.

Transcript: Treehouse Communities and the Rainbow Bridge

This client came to me just as she was starting to awaken and was making her way out of the Mormon community. She knew that she was meant for the New Earth and had concerns about whether her partner would be shifting too. She had been trying to have a baby and wasn't sure if she was meant to bring in a new child at this stage of the Ascension.

The client came into the scene and described herself as a light being above the Earth in space observing the planet. When I moved her forward, she saw herself now on the Earth resting by a beautiful waterfall. The client tells me that her heart is pounding as energy surges through her body.

C: The water is glowing like the stars, or like when you go to the ocean, and it has that glowy stuff when you walk. That's what it looks like, but it's coming down in a waterfall. And I'm just on the banks watching it, but it smells clean. And the stars are up; it is very beautiful. It's so beautiful.

M: Are you alone there, or are others with you?

C: Well, I am alone here, but I know there are people close. I'm just sitting there on a rock.

M: Do you sleep or eat?

C: I don't think so.

M: Feel into it. Tell me, how do you get your nourishment? How do you stay charged? Trust what comes to mind.

C: I feel like what I'm doing right now. Just sitting there. Oh yeah, there's an energetic exchange between the trees there and myself. It's basically like we are feeding each other kind of. It's just light...just energy, so just is.

M: So, there is some type of exchange? A relationship between the life force of the tree and yours?

C: Yeah, because it's the same thing. It's like a blue energy that I am feeling and seeing. It's also the same with the stars; it's the same with the water; it's the same thing that I look like.

M: What do you do with most of your time?

C: Right now, it feels like I would probably just want to play in the water. It feels like I am a keeper of the forest. I am. I know the trees and flowers and they know me. So, right now, I am walking in the forest. It's daytime now. It's so green! I am visiting with the plants. I'm touching them, talking to them. I can feel like I am more in a body now. I am female, yeah. I am just walking barefoot.

NEXT SCENE: EARTH COUNCIL MEETING

The client saw herself in a meadow next to an ocean. She was meeting a group of different intelligent beings in a council. She described two of the council members. One was blue with white-grey robes. Another was an insectoid, praying mantis-like being.

C: *I am in a long, white robe-y dress. This is like a council of some sort. We're gathering around now. It seems like very wise people, quiet people. There's not a lot of talking, just gathering around a table, but we're outside.*

M: Look around at these other beings around the table. Do you notice anything? What sticks out?

C: *Lots of non-human looking people, and some human-looking people as well. Somebody next to me looks like an elf with long, blonde hair, blue eyes, and white robes. We're sitting in these tall, straight-backed chairs. It seems very Lord of the Rings-esque (laughs). We are gathering a council.*

M: What is the purpose of this council?

C: *It's discussing Earth it seems like.*

M: What about Earth?

C: *What happens next. These people seem to be interested in a good part...let me think of how to say this. There seems to be a concern. Most have positive energy of wanting good. I'm sorry my heart is pounding so much. It's so strange because I feel like I am myself here.*

M: So, tell me what else you are learning at this council. What else is being talked about?

C: *So, I can only tap into a feeling. I am an advocate for humans. That is why I feel that I am there. I am holding space. I am very compassionate. I am still a female. I am feeling we're looking at planet Earth. It's like we're up in the sky looking at it. Let me see if I can feel these other people.*

M: What is happening where humans need an advocate? What's happening on the Earth?

C: So much sadness. There is a lot of pain (emotional). Some of these beings don't feel what humans can feel, but I can. And so, I am advocating for them, or speaking for them, that we can't abandon them. That is not right. It doesn't sit with my vibration, and the laws of the universe don't allow us to do that to them.

M: Why would they be talking about leaving humans alone? What happened?

C: Some feel that it's a lost experiment. To just let it be, let them destroy themselves. Other people know that cannot happen — that the planet cannot be destroyed. Some people would like to take away the veil, or the shield that leaves the humans in the dark.

Some are feeling that it's too soon and that humans couldn't handle that. I agree with them. It has to be incremental; it can't happen all at once. It seems unsafe; the chaos would intensify that they are not ready yet. I seem to want to advocate for the waking up of the human race. That keeping them shielded is not necessarily working like we hoped it would work.

M: Why did you shield the humans?

C: Well, we chose it. Humans chose it. We wanted it. It seems apparent to me that I am human.

M: Why would the human race choose to be shielded? Blocked off?

C: We wanted that lesson. Just like we learn as we become conscious and awake, we realize we chose it as a lesson. We needed that so we could wake up to it on our own. We needed to learn that internal shift, but what's happening is not many humans are finding that way back. They have gotten so lost. A lot of humans are really lost. We're discussing how we can have an awakening. How do we do this without removing the shield completely? Is it possible? It is what we are doing already; [it's] working because people are waking up, but not enough.

M: So, what will you do to help?

C: Oh, yes...oh, it's so interesting. Some don't want the experiment to end. That praying mantis insect doesn't see it as a negative, as a problem. The experiment, that's what it started out to be. It always was an experiment. Why would we deter from what is just naturally happening?

M: So, some are for the support of humans, and some don't see any reason for it.

C: Right, and it doesn't necessarily feel negative. It feels detached. I feel like this praying mantis does not understand emotion and cannot see why this is painful. Pain doesn't make sense. It's like watching bacteria grow sort of, he views it as just natural and interfering because of our emotions doesn't make sense. Emotions are very interesting. A lot of these people here don't understand emotions. And I am advocating for it, that is why we went to Earth. It created something for us.

M: What's happening now?

C: I just stood up. I am trying to explain something. Okay. They respect me. I look different. I am tall. I am standing at this table. I am not really talking. Basically, my heart chakra is just exploding out. I think I am trying to share with these beings why I chose to be a human, and this heart lesson, this chakra opening, I am pulsing out, and they are feeling the vibration of it.

M: How do they respond to the vibration?

C: A lot of them resonate. A lot of them understand already. It's interesting. Not all of these beings have the same chakras, maybe. It's different. And so, it doesn't necessarily resonate.

We're looking back on the Earth now. It seems the general, the majority of these people feel the same way I do. We want to help. Help is an interesting word, it's maybe not the right word. It's assistance.

M: How will you assist?

C: They already are. That's what is becoming very apparent to me. There is a lot of love that is being directed at that planet right now. Yeah, oh my goodness. It's...

M: It's strong, isn't it?

C: There is no worry anymore. They already decided. I am sort of seeing this Earth; it's very interesting.

M: What's so interesting, tell me.

C: It looks like a puzzle falling apart, sort of. Like it's blowing open and inside is just light. Ooh. But we're watching it. It's already happening. It's happening. We're kind of celebrating. There's a relief. I feel really drawn to it.

M: What's happening now?

C: Well, I see light, a lot of light coming from this core booming out. The old Earth looks like a puzzle piece that's floating away sort of. This is interesting; there is a light from the Sun. A huge sun, though.

M: What's happening with this light?

C: There's a beam; it's coming from the center of the Earth. It's matching up to this huge sun. It's like a welcoming; it's like part of the Sun. It's just becoming one with this light. It's just beaming. Being born. I'm sorry I don't have the words; it's just all really bright.

I'm zooming down to this light; I want to be in it. Bright blue-ish, white light. I have an image stuck in my head, and I can't really move forward. I think because I am actually observing it. I want to zoom into it, but I'm not.

M: What is the image?

C: It's an image of that huge sun and this planet just bright. It almost looks like a star. I'm observing it like I am in space.

M: Is this bright star the Earth?

C: Yes.

M: What's so interesting about this connection between the Earth and the Sun?

C: Ok, let me zoom out, actually. The Sun is just so huge. I can't see the whole, only a small part, but if I zoom out, I can see better...okay, yes, I can. There is a bridge, a connection between... Woah, I ...

M: Tell me about this bridge. What is it doing?

C: So, it looks like an electric current sort of, to me. There's an energy field around the Earth and the Sun, but they are connecting. Again, it's vague. It's like a tunnel kind of. It keeps trying to zoom from place to place. This is something that I've dreamt about already. It's this blue, the only way I can describe it is a wormhole like you would see in Star Trek. When they get in a wormhole and they're flying through this energy in blue light.

M: Where are you? Are you in the wormhole?

C: Yes, but I can choose it. It's so strange. I can zoom out and observe it in a different way. I can zoom in and be inside of it. My heart. In my dreams I always wake up before I get to the other side. It's getting brighter and brighter, so I just burst into this meadow.

M: What do you see there in the meadow?

C: Trees and it's so bright.

M: What else do you see there?

C: So, I am running and jumping really high, and I'm flying up in the sky. Amazing! I'm up in the sky, and I see mountains, then I just come back down to the meadow.

M: Is there anyone else there with you?

C: Not close, well, maybe. I kind of sense, again, I don't know if I am doing this right or if I am just making it up, but I definitely sense me. Just now me. And I am just jumping around and playing. I'm wearing this loose white dress, but it's short, so I can run. It's very flowy. But I sense my kids with me (laughing). I'm showing them. I am running and jumping into the sky and laughing and flipping around, and then they are doing it too.

M: Oh, wonderful, you're teaching them how to fly. What a joy. What else is happening?

C: I am observing my body. Oh, it's really beautiful (emotional). My skin is different. I am looking down and my stomach is healed. Strong. I can touch my skin; it's firm and browner. It's glowy.

NEXT SCENE: TREEHOUSE LIVING

C: Where I zoom to is a tree. A home in a tree. And I've heard this before, so I don't want to make it up; it's just what naturally happened when you said to change. It's a home in a tree. It's like stucco, or I want to say wood. Yeah, maybe wood. Oh, there are windows all around, and I can look out. There's an ocean out there, but there are trees all around me. There's a fireplace, which doesn't make sense to me at all (laughs). But I'm sitting there playing. There's a little girl (emotional). She has blonde, curly hair. She's wearing a white dressy-thing, rompy-thing. Oh, she has bright blue eyes! She's my little girl.

M: Look down at your body and tell me what you see about your body.

C: It's the same body that I was in at the meadow. Strong, healthy — very healthy — I have really long hair. Oh, this is so weird. I can sense that she's my baby, but I don't look like I've had a baby (laughs). I feel young, very healthy. Oh, I think...again, I don't know if I am making this up, I just looked in the kitchen and I saw my husband. Yes. It's our little girl.

M: So, you both made it to the New Earth.

C: Yes. Oh, it is so wonderful. I feel so happy. And my kids, they're outside. I have all my kids, and they're in the trees, swinging on vines and climbing up ladders, being crazy hooligans. But they're flying around, and I am not worried about them at all. They just are. They're with a bunch of other kids. If I look out my window, there are all these houses in trees, and there are just lights in the trees. And I feel completely whole because they are my family. It's all my family.

M: Why do you all build your homes in the trees?

C: It is just our natural place to be. That's just what came to mind. I don't understand it fully, because we just fly up there; we don't have to climb a ladder. The trees love us so much. They are holding us in their arms basically, and so it's our happiest place to be. That's where we want to be.

M: What are some other things about this new home for you? What's life like there?

C: My first observation is how I feel. I feel so complete. I don't feel scared for my kids. That's the first thing I am noticing — I don't feel scared for my children. They are completely safe and whole. I just get to enjoy them. Oh, now we're on the beach with a whole community — all people. We're dancing, playing music. Kids are so happy.

NEXT SCENE: NEW EARTH BABY

C: I am definitely pregnant. I have a baby inside of me growing. I am by a river. It's different than having a baby here; it's not riddled with pain, but, oh, it's different. It's still human. I'm still a human, and I'm still giving birth like a human. I'm surrounded by all sorts of beautiful things. Okay. Because we've recognized nature as technology almost, its intelligence; there's nature spirits and trees and animals. And we don't need hospitals and things like that because we understand nature so much, so it's completely safe and beautiful. It's technology. That blue light that I always see in the water and in the trees, it's some form of really advanced technology, but it's what we would call "nature" (laughs). I know that doesn't make any sense, really...

So, nature is technology. It's coming and holding the baby as I birth it, and I am breathing in this blue energy from the water and the air and the trees, which immediately heals my body, and the baby is immediately just healthy.

M: So, if you don't get sick there, if you're healed so easily, how long will you live?

C: Oh, my goodness. I feel like I could live forever. I would choose, probably, if I wanted to live that forever, I don't think I would age unless I chose it. Oh! Just, I was observing that scene from such a kind of scientific observation, watching this energy exchange, and then, all of a sudden, I realized that is my baby (emotional). That's my baby.

M: How wonderful to receive this gift.

WORKING WITH THE HIGHER SELF

HS: There is energy right now coming from the Sun to the Earth. Some are calling it "The Event." This is what we were showing her.

M: Can you tell us more about this process and how it's going to happen?

HS: It is already happening. More and more feel it. It's coming in waves. This bridge is...it looks like a bridge between the Sun and the Earth; it's a bridge between New Earth and Old Earth. The energy from the Sun is what is creating that bridge.

M: How can we work with these waves in a way that supports our evolution?

HS: Just by choosing to incarnate at this time, you chose to work with it. You don't really need to do anything at this point. It's happening. If you are here on the planet now, then you already made your choice, and you will feel this. There is no way to escape. If you want to enhance it, continue your personal raising of vibration. But even with that, even without that, everyone will feel it.

M: Can you tell us more about the experiment with the humans?

HS: I think that to humans, sometimes it can feel cold, detached. It is a form of experiment, but humans actually chose it. People here right now chose to be a part of the experiment. The experiment, it's not as horrible as it sounds. It's actually very beautiful. It's an experiment of consciousness, of vibration. That is all any of this is. An experiment, all an experience, which is an experiment. You can feel the human as a piece of the experiment, of experience, a piece of consciousness. If you can pull out of feeling like this is all there is, then you can view yourself, your Higher Self, the completion of you not as a human experience. It's just a piece of it. So, if you can do that, if you can pull out of that, you understand that an aspect of yourself wanted to learn lessons that could only be experienced in coming to planet Earth.

M: What was happening in Earth or human history that made us choose this way of being? This disconnect? Was it always like this?

HS: It has not always been like this. If you take yourself back in human history, way, way, way back to some of the lost cities when humans chose to descend into the third dimension, they did not understand the consequences. They did not know what it would feel like. They didn't know the disconnect from Source.

That's why it's called an experiment. It was unknown. They chose it for lessons to be learned, and as some of these humans are waking up — as you call it — do you not feel excited about the lessons you are learning? **(M: Yeah.)** *That's why you did it (smiles). Reconnecting with Source — you've always been connected to Source but remembering your connection to Source is one of the reasons you came.*

M: What are some of the other reasons?

HS: Third density, the third dimension, is the lowest frequency. This planet is the lowest vibration planet. We wanted to know what the third density felt like. It was not and isn't associated with something negative. It's not that. It's something new in the universe that some of us wanted to feel. Brave souls.

M: So now that she has this information, how does this apply to her life?

HS: What we want her to do is to grasp her power of conscious creation. Playing with it right now in her life. We want her to become a master manifester, a manipulator of energy; we want her to know that she has the power fully — and always has — we want her to remember. Wake up!

Transcript: New Earth Treehouse

This client is the same who brought forward the Master Alchemist life scenes. It is interesting how some of the same themes show up multiple lifetimes. Let us travel to New Earth and learn more about the civilization.

C: It's very futuristic. There's flying vehicles. Buildings are shaped uniquely. It's beautiful. There's activity but not too much activity. There's something about it that looks like wonderland. There's a theme park here that has rollercoasters. I don't know, there's something about it that makes me feel like it's fun, like wonderland. It's colorful. Buildings aren't just clean and boring. Some are just like clean color, like off-white, but then there's bits of colors and tubes and things.

M: Look down at your body and tell me what you notice.

C: Woman's feet. And again, in a thong shoe sort of. [I'm wearing] somewhat like a sari, because it has beautiful silk and colors, and sort of the way it's wrapped, but it's loose too. It feels so good to wear it. I love the way it moves around my body, very flowing, like I'm flowing.

M: Are you holding anything?

C: It's a silver rod, like a sparkling silver rod in my right hand. It's not a torch...there's something about the top of it that reminds me of the torch on the Statue of Liberty, but it's smaller, like a wand more. Cadu...caduceus?

M: What do you use it for?

C: My magic! (giggles)

M: What kind of magic do you do with it?

C: I make beautiful things, everywhere. Beautiful. People like the spaces I make for them to live in. I can make anything, but I like to make art out of clothing. It funnels my energy and abilities, just like in the pyramid that I showed previously. And it funnels through, except I'm sort of the crystal. There is a crystal in it, in the top. That's why it has that top to it, okay. Like, the top of the pyramid is like what I hold in my hand, and I am like a receiver. Yeah, like I'm like the top and it goes through me, yes, and then I can distribute it in smaller measures, and use control with it to create things. Like a paintbrush.

NEXT SCENE: HER TREEHOUSE

C: (Giggles) Oh, I love it. It's a giant tree, but I have built it. You walk up to the giant tree and there are flowers everywhere. It's like the shell of a snail, that material, so it doesn't hurt the tree, right? And it wraps around the tree, going up, not tightly like the snail, but like you would walk around a circular staircase. And it's all beautiful colors, so the light, when you first go it's like the darker shell, but as you go up it becomes like a lighter seashell color, and the sunlight and everything can go through it. The light can go right through it and illuminates. Oh, and there are holes, like windows, but you don't need glass or anything.

So, as you walk up the spiraling staircase you have the holes and you can see down over the community because I'm on top of a hill, on a big tree. Because I do live off of my own, I come and go. I go into the village and in the town and create things for people and work with other artists, but I always go back to my own space. And it goes up and I can see the town and I can see the water, like the beach. We all like to go to the beach.

The vines and all the flowers, they droop and hang inside and outside, and then I go up and...I can make it really high because there's no rush and I don't get tired going up stairs (laughs). I enjoy every step and I enjoy the view every single step, and so it's great that it's high up. I could just fly up, and I do sometimes. I don't have to take the stairs (laughs), but sometimes I like to take the stairs.

And then, yeah, it just opens up and oh, it's just so open. And the view, it's like the shell kind of just expands out around the tree and through the different branches that form off. I can travel around, and the monks don't even like...it's open so that the birds and animals can just come and go.

NEXT SCENE: EATING IN HER HOME

C: *Flowers! (laughs) They just grow right in my kitchen. I have these big windows all around. It reminds me of the starship Voyager, where they have these big, oval windows where you can look out to space, well, it's like that but they're just open. So, it's just like these big, beautiful flowers that are just so voluptuous and big, and they grow right in there, just for the pleasure of me eating them. I don't really need anything else, like vegetables and berries and things, you know, but some things just grow right to me. They just grow right to my room, and I can just take them and pick them and eat them, or I can make things with them like salads that you might want to share with people.*

I don't really cook food anymore, but there's like a preparation area because we like to prepare food together sometimes. If I'm just eating myself, then I just eat my things, but when other people come, they will bring things like the flowers that grow for them in their space, or vegetables. They bring the things that grow for them because it's a reciprocal energy process that they exchange with the plants so, you know, in essence it's like part of their consciousness and their energy goes into these plants and it's like this sharing thing and so when they bring them over, that's why we would make a salad, because everyone brings their own energy in with the food that we bring, and then we share it together and it's just even more wonderful. Yes.

M: Wow, nice. Does anybody eat meat?

C: *No. (Giggling) No. (Strongly)*

M: Well, when you have food coming to you like that, I can see why.

C: *Oh, no. You wouldn't hurt anything or anything like that. If you want a flower that tastes like steak, you can have a flower that tastes like steak. You don't need to eat a rabbit! (Laughing) Leave the poor thing alone! No. They sleep with me! They're all around everything. Even animals that I wouldn't have around me here now, I enjoy their company — we communicate, we laugh together.*

I'm not going to eat one of my friends! (Laughing) And I'm not going to let anyone else eat my friends. Nobody does that.

M: Friends don't let friends eat friends.

C: Friends don't let friends eat friends. No, silly. We're all laughing at that right now around the table. It's like you're there, too, like you're there on the TV, and we're all sitting and having this conversation with you; we're sitting and laughing at the joke of it.

M: What was it like for everyone there at the table to make the transition to this place?

C: Blink of an eye. Poof! It's magic (laughing). One of them even went poof, like a cartoon, just like poof! It's magic, and one of them just made sparkles (giggles).

M: Does anyone there have a story about what the transition was like? What was happening before the magic came in?

C: John says that he will share his story. So he was in the city, on the pavement, in the street, and everyone is just going about their business, talking on their cellphones, and then he feels a prickle in the air...but it's like, because the trickling and intensity is building, and he's going "Is this it? Is this it?" It keeps getting stronger and when he starts to feel the prickling, he's like "Is this it?" But then it just keeps getting stronger. He's like "Ok, I'm definitely not dreaming now." He stomps his foot on the pavement; he had a newspaper in his hand.

M: And so, what was it like after his skin started to prickle up?

C: Like a bright flash, just whoosh, flash! And everyone was like 'woah!' and dropped to the ground like stones. Nothing is working. Nothing is working. Nothing is working. John says he's still with me, still sitting at the table.

M: Ok, what does John want to say?

C: Well, so, it's a bright flash. Like you can see, just like in the animations, like a ring flash around so bright that everyone's blinded, but as they get up and start blinking their eyes they realize okay, the phones aren't working, cars aren't working, traffic lights aren't working. The lights are all off. So, they're all so focused on the technology that they're not noticing the cloud, but as soon as the technology is off, I'm like okay, that's pointless. I know it's not going to work; there's no point, so I look up. Everyone is looking down and around. They only start to look up when the sky starts to get dark. At first it seems like when a thunderstorm starts to come in, like when everything gets dark because the clouds are dark, but it's touching down on the atmosphere, and that's when they start to run.

M: Where do they run?

C: Everywhere (laughs). Amok! But John just sat there. He was like okay, there's no point in going anywhere. Anywhere. He was sitting down already, and he considered that a blessing. He was ready to go, and he knew what to do. So, he just went in. He went in, in preparation, and tuned out all of the people running around, but he's not the only one. There's someone by a fountain that sits, in a green shirt. Somebody gets out of the car and sits down on the ground. Someone else just lies down on the ground, away from the people running around. So, he's not the only one. And there's an awareness of each other too, so it's time, and there's a unified energy. As it comes closer, it's purple, and as it breaks through it's like rainbow electricity breaking through the sphere almost as if rainbow lightning were to go across the top of a sky. But the purple clouds, okay, waving up and that's what it is, so it is...there's a joining of when the light hits; it did touch down and activate something at the center of the Earth. It did. So, it's not just that it's coming; it's the meeting of the two energies that causes the wave. Pulse in, zap, activate, pulse out, out from the center of the Earth out to the atmosphere, and when those touch each other, that's when the wave spills over, and that's why it's so massive. All the way it's so massive that the city buildings that I was around even seem puny. Like if it was a thunderstorm, the buildings would block out some of those dark clouds, but it minimizes everything.

M: So, what happens next?

C: It comes, like a wall. So, as he sees it, he's sitting in a cemented area, there are some stairs going down, there's like a large building with stairs going down, and the wave comes and reaches the faces of the buildings that are closest to him, like a wall of the ocean, like when Moses parted the seas, it approaches. And as it approaches, he just closes his eyes. He just lets it come.

M: And so, what happens after it comes?

C: A wall of energy that you just almost dissolve into color and sound...truth... remembrance, and... the bliss of love.

M: What happens to the physical body?

C: It disintegrates. Like sand...but not lost. It's like if I were to look at cells of the 3D body, they turn to sand in this reality, but in that, they become like clear bubbles, crystal-clear bubbles of light and energy. So, once they were a dry thing, now it is like fluid, like water, crystalline and pure. The great alchemy of turning sand into water, sort of. It's a transfiguration. So, what falls away and disintegrates is like the outer shell of this 3D form, but it transmutes and comes alive in essence. It sheds the old, dead idea.

M: What about the other people? What happens to them, the ones that were running?

C: *Taken. They were taken away. They were taken on the ships.*

M: Where to?

C: *Healing. Preparation. They will be returned to the Earth. So, they are taken somewhere unconsciously. They are not all consciously aware. Not all are returned. Some are returned. Some are kept, healed, and helped, and able to transfer on. Some not as yet and are returned to carry on with their story. They cannot unplug from the concepts of 3D. Their ego is fighting way too hard, so it's not their time yet. There are those of us that are just able to... that's what we came here to do, so we are able and prepared to transmute instantly. So, with that comes the great knowing, with the great knowing comes access to any information needed in that moment of now, so you just know where to go.*

M: Do you stay on that version of Earth?

C: *No. We go to where we are now; we go to the New Earth now. Yes. Done with that now. We did our grid holding up until the moment that the wave arrived, we plugged in, like we talked about before, the tent pegs were held in, we held it in, put the stakes down, that was our job. We can go back and forth if we want to, to teach and carry missions but we don't have to go back in that form, and that's what will help others because they need their miracles.*

All Roads Lead Home

There are as many pathways to New Earth as there are people. Once "the shift" happens, everyone will move to where their next evolutionary phase will play out. Stay in your heart. Stay with your breath and trust your footing as you walk towards this new reality.

EIGHT

New Earth Civilization

When I worked with Neomi, I always cued for her to go to the most appropriate place for our learning. Most often, Neomi would often go to the same lifetime of Esther, the Essene. On a few occasions, we would get a surprise. Let us journey with her to the New Earth

M: What do you see as you look around? What comes to mind?

C: Like a rocky cliffside with trees and I'm way, way, way high up on the cliffside. Below me, down below in the distance, is a town. I don't feel...not really in a human form. I'm like a bird. I'm feathered and a bluish coloring. I'm the size of a human and I'm male. I feel like it's my job to observe over this small...well, it's a medium-size village. It seems that humans are living down below. So, my job is to watch over them and make sure nothing comes into sight or discovers their location. It's somewhat like a desert there. It's really rocky and sandy, but there are trees here and there. Down in the village area where the people are, there's grass and bushes and things, but I just live in this sliced-out side of the cliff. I don't have anything in this space where I live. It's just my duty to sit there and watch over them.

M: How long have you been doing this?

C: I feel like I've been doing this a long time, like maybe twenty years or thirty years. I'm to look out for things coming in via the sky, so just like anything from up in the heavens or anything. What will happen on occasion is that an aircraft will come in, and it's cylindrical like a disc. I'm to alert the people. I'm to fly down, and there's a designated person in the village that I'm to inform. That's my duty. It doesn't come very often, but as soon as it's in the air, I'm to alert them. It doesn't seem to be dangerous. It's as if I'm informing them so that they can then coordinate with the aircraft.

M: What does the aircraft do once it's here? Why are they coordinating with them?

C: It comes down, and it will pick up the human beings on occasion and it just comes in broad daylight, in the middle of the afternoon. I'll go ahead and let them know they're here. It's a valley they are in, so the spaceship has to land on

the other side of this...kind of like a foothill of a mountain. So then just a handful of people will travel over to the spacecraft and then they will leave. Then after some time, it's usually a long duration, usually seven or eight months, they bring them back, and they return. It's different people that go at different times. It's as if they are supposed to be going for a training. They go to train and then come back.

I believe they're training the beings that are coming in on the aircraft. They're going back to where they reside, and then the humans train them in what they do...like as to be human and about emotions, and they explain to them how they live. But it's odd they don't stay here... They take the humans with them and then bring them back. It seems it would be much more efficient training if they stayed here to train, but they don't.

M: Do the humans also get trained?

C: When they leave, they are attuned to different energy systems. When they come back, they have more skills as far as telepathy and energetic skills...so that they can elevate objects using energy from their mind. So, there is an exchange. I feel like this isn't too radically off into the future from the present time. I feel like this is just like maybe 200 or 300 years in the future.

There's one other person...I'm not sure what to call myself...that is like a...like a bird person that lives in a cutout opposite me across this valley. So, the both of us do this, but there are no other beings like us that are around. I don't feel like there are any other humans anywhere near us. I'm not quite sure if there are any other humans on Earth besides this settlement.

M: What kind of structures are in this settlement?

C: It's just small houses. So, it's set up like a village. They're built with a lot of silver material, and it just seems like there's...it's slightly futuristic... So, it's like silver roofs and the walls are white, but it's not like siding or anything. It's almost like a plastic white exterior. There are paths in between the people's houses. They come out and they interact throughout the day.

They do have gardens and things. I don't see any animals around. There are no birds or anything. It's just the humans living here. So, it looks like they're able to provide for themselves with the gardens that they have. They're just wearing very simple clothes, just like robes or whatnot. They just have a tie at the waist, so they're dressed very simply. They have sandals and that. They gather regularly to eat. They eat in their homes, but sometimes they'll gather outside. But they're very, very peaceful people. They do seem to keep records a *lot. There is one building that serves as a library, and so they're always going in, and they're scribing different information. So, I'm not sure if they're recording information from their own knowledge or...I'm not clear what they're recording. So, they go in and out, and sometimes they have groups that come in and talk amongst themselves, just kind of learning and having meetings.*

But I don't know exactly what they're talking about because I'm not involved. I can see in when they open the doors and that, but I really don't get a break or anything like that. I'm really to watch out and protect them as well.

M: When do you get to Earth? Or how?

C: I was brought in on the ship by the beings that are bringing them in. I was from another planet. Our planets communicate with each other. So, there are more like me on my planet. We can talk telepathically...all of us...and it was deemed by the Council that just the two of us bird men [would] come in and watch over and then be a contact point between the humans and the beings that come in.

We have many agreements in the planets that are outside of this galaxy...the Earth galaxy and the Milky Way. There are many others, so we communicate amongst ourselves. The different planets...there's the Council so they set up information...it's not as far-fetched as it seems to be in the human's mind to go to other planets and travel because we have modes of transportation that...I can't fly to other planets. We can go into vehicles and get to other planets to have meetings or collaborate on things that we need to do. And I had volunteered for this position. They had asked, and I accepted.

M: How did you first get in contact with Earth?

C: Well, the Council makes decisions sometimes, so sometimes things need to be done, or the humans have needed assistance over the years, and so the council will...they're not to interfere, they can only send and assist and honestly, hope for the best sometimes. So, I was approached this time, other times you have your resting period, and you can go to Source and re-energize yourself. Some people that come to Earth, they're just so exhausted, it really takes everything out of them, and they need a long time to rejuvenate and re-energize. But others, it doesn't take very long, just a mini vacation or something and then beings are ready to come back. So, then you're just able to submit that request to council and then decide what your journey will be. Or, if it needs to be...if they need anything done. They need volunteers a lot.

So, I usually always volunteer. I love serving so I ask them what their needs are and then we incorporate that into my lifetimes. It kind of makes...it's more fun that way. I get to have...so I'll serve a purpose that they deem necessary, but then also sprinkle in, sometimes, say like in my human lifetimes...you know...just regular human problems. Kind of mixes it up.

But there's been some things happening over the years...so the Earth was very sick for a long time, so a lot of destruction happened. So now we've arrived at this small village...this small group of people... It's not a small group, there's...I would say there's a few hundred people down there. So, they are re-establishing themselves, and they're going to go ahead and grow again. So, it's going to be a slow process, but I think everything has been weeded out so that there isn't the destruction and the heavy darkness and the violence. All of those just heavy, heavy low energies spread all over the Earth. That...with these people...it will be able to grow and flourish again as a healthy planet.

M: You said, "weeded out." What happened to the rest of the humans?

C: They just weren't ready for the transition. Some just didn't accept...just have faith and truly accept the information that they were given. I don't really mean weeded out in a bad way. There were many, many beings that were just on a self-destructive path...so they were...those lives were terminated. But there were others that...they had faith, but they just weren't strong. They didn't have a true faith, and so they had to be relieved of their lifetime and go back to Source, for now. So slowly...hopefully...those souls will re-energize and reset, and with this slow growth of the planet, then they'll be reintroduced to the planet, or possibly other planets.

But everything went spiraling out of control, so it just had to end. There were many, many, many people that survived. It's just that with the destruction, some people didn't end up surviving, per se...as far as being able to survive from a survival standpoint. They lived through it, but they weren't able to collaborate and thrive. So now it's...the people that were able to, have collaborated into this village. There were people that thrived for quite a while, but just...then they just didn't collaborate in groups. So then, as they passed, their smaller groups died out.

M: What made this group so successful at surviving?

C: They just collaborated together. They realized that they needed to come together and set up a peaceful place to live and start up their gardens...rally all of their resources and knowledge to thrive in a healthy manner. So, nothing that will be in a...like pollute the Earth or anything like that. With all the destruction and what happened, the Earth was wiped clean. So, it was...it was made rid of all of the pollution that the humans had built up over hundreds of years. So that was able to be removed, and so now this group is starting...and the smaller groups did too...with a clean new Earth.

So, with this new Earth, they need to respect it, and they're aware of that. So, they're very careful to put their resources...to gather water, grow with the gardens...store things in a very responsible manner because they're understanding of what happened in the past. That may be part of what they're scribing, so it doesn't happen again in the future.

NEXT SCENE: INCOMING CRAFT

C: *Ok, now there are numerous...numerous aircraft coming in, and they are landing along the outside of this valley where the humans are living. They've brought, each craft has brought maybe eight or ten people, so they're bringing them back and bringing new people in adult form. So...I'm not...I don't have the information of how that's happening, but they're bringing in new people to integrate but they're already adults. So, people who were not here previously. They're just re-integrating them into this group. The group seems very receptive. It seems like they know these people. They're embracing and hugging them like they were expecting them, but it's just interesting because they're already coming in adult form as if they're being adopted. So, the people who have already lived here have built new houses for these newcomers to reside in. So, it looks like they're expanding the population, but I don't have the information on how they're, you know, mysteriously bringing these adult humans back here. So that's fascinating. But they're embracing them and very peaceful.*

It seems like the alien, well, the extraterrestrial beings are coming in, and prior...years and years back, they were not able to leave the aircraft, but now they can come out of the aircraft and walk around and speak with the humans as well. And they can speak to them as if...nobody's alarmed to see them. So, I don't know if, over time, they developed the skills to be able to withstand the surface of the Earth and the atmosphere. It seems prior to this they were not able to.

M: Why weren't they able to?

C: *The Sun was just way too harsh and radiant and just the air alone would burn their skin. So, they just couldn't...it's almost like they couldn't stand the light as* *well. Well, they came from...it's a rocky, craggy planet and it's really dark. It's very dark and grey. They talk telepathically and that, but it's very...if a human went there, they'd say it's depressing. It's all monochrome. It's just one grey color kind of, just shades of grey. And the beings themselves are a blue-grey color themselves as well. And it's dim. And the air there is very dry and there's no humidity. So, I think when they came to Earth the humidity was irritating to them and like I said...the Sun, they just couldn't stand the rays.*

Now the extraterrestrial beings...they're talking with the humans, and they're greeting them and everyone's happy that this is happening. I think, possibly, this is the first time this has happened and they're really happy that this is a successful venture, and I'm starting to get the feeling that the humans they brought in are the extraterrestrial beings and they were able to morph into a human form so they could live on the planet and integrate in. But you can't tell the difference between the native Earth person and the extraterrestrial Earth person, so I'm not sure. I'm not getting a read on why they are doing this because it seems like the village has grown in the past few years and everything is thriving and healthy.

Neomi finishes her mission as the bluebird being and returns to Source and the council where she enthusiastically volunteers to reincarnate on the Earth as a human in the new colony. She mentioned that there was less to prepare for because Earth did not have the low-vibrational experiences anymore and that it was simply about building up the new society. In that new life, she was trained by a Christ Conscious Avatar, a very high, divine being who was also living in the community. She commented on how successful the new civilization was growing and that many new babies were being born on the Earth in pristine, high-frequency birthing temples to ensure the happiness and health of the future generations. Mission complete!

Transcript: Culmination of the Divine Mission

When Laura came into the scene, she described a crystal pyramid which refracted rainbow light. Other pyramids and crystalline structures spread out around her. All of the life forms were etheric and radiant. She described herself being a Lightbody form of a feline humanoid wearing a gossamer fabric gown and carrying a crystal tablet filled with information from her soul's Akashic records. I asked for her to tune into the data and tell me what she was reading from the tablet.

C: *It is referring to this time in the present moment. It speaks of the leonine energies embodying in this timeline on this planet, in this new creation for the evolution of the planet, the overturning of the old ways — the birthing of the new. It's a very exciting time. It's a very noble time. It's a very expansive time for humanity to awaken out of their slumber, to come to full consciousness of the radiance of the divinity of who we are as a collective. It seems there are thousands or many hundreds of thousands of beings from different star seeds, different planets working together — for this momentous time. And, apparently, it is drawing nearer.*

M: **When you say it's drawing nearer, what do you mean by that? What do you see there?**

C: *I hear the word culmination — the culmination of a great many efforts and plans and meetings and battles, and victories ongoing in the cleanup of the old ways — the old consciousness. A step up — it's a step up for all of creation. Yeah…it's, it's on its way.*

NEXT SCENE: MEETING WITH COUNCIL OF ELDERS

C: *I am in a meeting with the Council of Elders. There is a discussion on what is progressing and how things have progressed, and they are very pleased with how things are moving forward and relieved. It's been a hard, intricate strategy to awaken mankind and to deliver mankind from the clutches of dark entities — the shadow consciousness. They were uncertain at some point in the timelines, but victory is the Light's. Victory is the Light's.*

M: **When you look around at this Council, tell me about them.**

C: *Babaji. Yogananda. Mother Mary. Sananda [Jesus]. There are some of the Kumaras there. St. Germain and other beings from other star systems that I don't know.*

M: **Well, what else is the Council sharing? Tell me what's happening now.**

C: *Making ready to advance humanity in the recognition of and welcoming of other advanced civilizations to promote humanity finally into the galactic community. Humanity needed to recognize the great play and deceit and turn away their attention from the attempted dramas, and over time they have done this in a noble way — opening their intuitive reckonings in their hearts and reaching in to remembering that we are not alone, and as...and when they have reached this tipping point in the collective, they have lost or released their fear of the star beings.*

And there is a part of them that remembers that they, too, are star beings, and they too have lived in many realms and dimensions and planets and cultures and civilizations. They have come to a place of being open to living amongst and with the star brethren as equals — not as lost children, but as equals in the eyes of all our galactic brothers and sisters. And this is part of the work the Council and many, many other councils have engaged in over the decades to prepare mankind for this evolutionary outcome and shift towards the galactic ingathering.

M: It sounds like we've been working a long time to get to this place — to be right at the tipping point.

C: It started 2,000 years ago — the seeds were planted in the Age of Pisces for the dawning of the Age of Aquarius. And in the late 18th century, people were impulsed, having come out of the Dark Ages, to bring the Light forward — upwards, the knowledge of spirituality, the knowledge of esoteric traditions — to start impulsing, planting seeds, and awakening mankind and we are right in the cusp.

M: So, what needs to happen before we move into that shift point? How close are we?

C: It's like a great cosmic computer is set. The program is set. The program is running, and we are in the process — we have been, but that process is speeding up infinitely now with the Earth and her creatures and inhabitants. She is moving; she is readying herself for the full mass ejection of Light from the Cosmic Center. It's like the image of a racehorse at the starting gate waiting for the bell to go — waiting for the boom to lift. There's a great sense of anticipation, excitement to have more and more of the collective wake up, to have that quantum energy excel and expand — quantum consciousness. So, the energies coming in keep impulsing more and more people. The whole of the planet is being impulsed — it's like electrodes just pulsing and pulsing and pulsing, and people's awareness is shifting rapidly towards this culmination of the Light.

M: Very good. Is there anything else that the Council would like to share? What would they like to talk with us about?

C: They say we are...we are well pleased. We are well pleased. Everything is flowing according to the great galactic ascension. All eyes are on the Earth for she is the pearl of the universe, and that pearl will become the diamond — the radiant diamond — the radiant sun in her own right. As she ascends, they watch with eagerness and an excited tension, rapt attention to monitor everything that is transpiring for things to stay the course. And for those starseeds to step forward and radiate — continue to radiate their magnificent Light and Love, to be the beams of Light as they have been and more of them to come out of their hiding to grab their courage and their will and come forward, and to be themselves in their true divinity — whether they are to be themselves, and also to exhibit and attend to their life plan and purpose amongst mankind.

M: What makes the difference between the average human and the starseeds? What's the difference between them?

C: The starseeds have remembered who they are. They have come in more awake and with the remembrance of their life plans and their purpose, and the regular humans have taken much longer in their evolutionary process to awaken in the sense that they, in the same way, have volunteered to only awaken at certain times in order for this drama to perpetuate. A much deeper will and desire for the Light in its perfect place and perfect time. Everyone has had their divine purpose planned as such, and their awakenings planned according to the Grand Design. The Light and the Dark needed to play off each other.

NEXT SCENE: EARTH IN THE FUTURE

C: I am in some sort of community building. It's like a school. And I am training to lead and teach young children. And we go out on nature excursions, and we do many things with learning to manifest at will, to use our minds to create, to project, and receive messages — telepathy. To learn to be in tune with all species on the planet, to communicate and receive direction and healing from everyone and everything. It's very beautiful.

M: That sounds very beautiful. What do you call this planet that you are on now?

C: This is Earth. This is Earth in the future. Two hundred years from now. We can teleport. We can avail ourselves of great healing...technologies. We can be anywhere we choose at any time.

M: And how are you able to travel to any place at any time? What is the experience like?

C: Well, there have been antigravity machines for some time now so we can travel in those, and when we learn to teleport, we can transport our bodies from one place to the next.

M: That's very nice. What else is happening there that you can do now?

C: Communities come together. There is a great deal of sharing. There's a great deal of building together. There's a great deal of support and sharing and creative endeavors that belong to everyone, as everyone shares in its creation — whatever that means, whatever that looks like that smaller communities need. Everyone works together. There's a great deal of cooperation and sharing.

M: What did it take to get to that point on the planet?

C: As every portal came opened, more light — higher frequencies — the resonance and magnetic gauss on the planet — shifting and changing — there were many timelines collapsing into a more unified field where people's hearts, wills, intentions, and desires are aligning into one collective consciousness and unconditional love and unconditional vision. And then there was the wave that came from the Galactic Center to harmonize, to shift — to transport the Earth into the higher timeline and density. And it has taken some years for certain people to be impulsed to bring through technologies, a new way of building homes, new ways of utilizing energy, a new way of healing, a new way of eating, and technologies were brought forward from the star brothers and sisters to cleanse the earth, to cleanse the waters, to cleanse the air, and to re-impregnate the earth with vital minerals that the topsoil was totally stripped of.

So, it has taken decades to pull this all through everyone working together for the highest good of the planet and the collective. And each generation and each decade has moved through in a purposeful way and purposeful consciousness and direction, vision — to open up this new civilization, and working together with star brothers and sisters. in cooperation with them, to accept their technologies, and to learn from each other, and to work and play with each other, and grow with each other and harmonize with each other. It's taken many decades, and it is flowing, and it has flowed and will continue to flow beautifully, peacefully, harmoniously, productively. And everyone experiences a great deal of prosperity, happiness, creativity, and joy, and play.

M: And speaking of play, tell me more about the educational systems. You said you were working with children and learning telepathy and things like this. What else is sticking out about the educational systems?

C: Children begin to learn about technologies that are being used, enhancements with technologies for the highest and greatest good of all. It starts out simply with very simple dynamics of say antigravity machines — the coils, the metals, minerals that are used as the conductive materials, their qualities. Crystals — the healing power of crystals — pulling through all of the elements of Earth and the universe. Bring them all together so the children can learn to...how to use these, to understand them and to grow with them so that technology is a commonplace. Learning to access the Akashic fields so that they remember who they are...they remember their lifelines, timelines. They know who they are in Spirit...they can connect with that part of themselves very easily, education.

M: How do you help these kids tune in to the Akashic fields? What's an exercise that you do with them? See it now.

C: They ask a question in their minds, and they learn to drop their conscious awareness down into their heart space, and they look for symbols, colors, and messages. They learn — they are trained to learn to listen. They are trained to learn to go into the still, quiet space — a very deep, deep space in the heart to hear the answers quite naturally, to see the answers, to feel them, hear them. Use all their inner senses — inner taste, inner smell. They ask the question, and they go down into a very deep place like a zero point where all things are known. All things are revealed to heighten their intuition. They have to go into these meditative places. The more they do this, the more they are able to access the Akash. It becomes second nature for them because they are young, and they are open — this is why they are trained at a young age.

NEXT SCENE: COMMUNITY COUNCILS

C: For each community, there is a group of people who monitor and supervise and watch the communities, watch their particular community. And so, I see in a room a group of people evaluating processes, evaluating how the community is doing — if there are any queries or questions if anything comes up. These people are elected to work through these and to find solutions for the best and highest good of all concerned. And these change periodically so that there is a — so there is equal opportunity for everyone to sit in the committee to lead the community, to have their say to work on different issues or any issues that come up, to resolve them and to learn and grow from them as a teaching method for all. And in this way, everyone participates; there's no hierarchy; there is equal participation with everyone in the community.

M: And how is it that people are selected? How is it decided by the people?

C: It is circular in the sense that it's a round table. Everyone has an opportunity to be at the table. Everyone has an opportunity to have voted in the first ten to twenty people. And it's like there is a roster where everyone has their chance. As soon as that table has completed their term, the next table comes up.

NEXT SCENE: COMMUNITY FIRE GATHERINGS

C: I see this huge fire. There is a massive fire pit, and there's this huge fire that is built in this large temple. There are many people. Many people coming from many communities in the area, and they...it's an ingathering, a harvesting of fruits and vegetables and produce that people bring as an honoring in the old ways to Mother Earth. It's the sacred time of the year where many communities come together to share what they have, to offer what they have, to respect Mother Earth, to respect the elements — the elementals. In a way even though we are in the future — we as humans remember how important it is to appreciate Mother Earth; and this is a very beautiful, sacred ceremony by the elders, by the children, by the young people to glorify, to deify, to appreciate, and to honor the bounty of Mother Earth throughout all the eons, throughout all the civilizations — the culmination of all the ages.

It is very beautiful, and everyone is laughing and singing and dancing and sharing the light of the fire — the energy of the fire. Singing to Mother Earth and really celebrating this culture — this new age, and our ancient roots and connection to Mother Earth.

M: What do you see there as you look around the celebration? What's it like there?

C: The feeling is of deep, deep gratitude, deep reverence — a holiness. People hold the gratitude and appreciation in their hearts. People gravitate towards each other and mingle and mix, and exchange gifts and things they have created as a gesture of goodwill and humanity that just knows no boundaries; just unconditionally loves and shares — coming together — circles of light, of love, of joy; time away from the regular day-to-day life — just a holiday. There's singing and music, and the children play.

M: Sounds perfect there.

C: Yes, it is. It's beautiful. The love is palpable.

HIGHER SELF CONVERSATION

M: When we were talking about disclosure and us returning to our connection with our star families and being able to travel across time and space, do you have anything else you would like to share with us about those subjects?

C: (Laughs) It's such an amazing time for all of humanity to realize our destiny amongst the star beings — our homes, all the homes we have come from — and that there is the opportunity for beings to travel wherever and whenever they wish. That opportunity is coming, and that is so exciting for mankind. This is such a great turning — such a great time, and that excitement is what needs to propel both this one and many others to excel in their work, in their light, in their beingness, and their sharing with the rest of humanity.

M: Do you have suggestions to help us get through these times?

C: We say find quiet times. Set your intention to receive with each portal with each new astrological event, with each new waking day. The new Light codes that come through are bringing through all of those abilities, which need to be integrated, which is why there is a repeated call for rest, lots of water, lots of fresh food and meditation, exercise, yoga. To really prepare the body, the mind, the heart for all these abilities that are coming through to each individual as and when they are ready to receive them. Their vessels need to be ready to receive these gifts, and this is why the call for care of the physical bodies is so vitally important. Just to take care of ourselves in the sweetest way as we grow and expand, and like we can nourish ourselves all the way through this.

And appreciation of the body. The body is the temple. The body is the vessel. The body is the housing to integrate, align all that is physically, emotionally, mentally, spiritually — so aligning all those aspects and keeping...keep calling into alignment those aspects into the body, into the incarnation, into this timeline, into this presence. As a daily, perhaps hourly practice — and cleansing, smudging, cleansing — calling in the I AM Presence to cleanse the bodies, because there are still energies out there that are untoward. And so, calling for Spirit to ensure the energy bodies and the energy field is clear, strong — any openings or any aberrations to be healed, cleared, and strengthened and transformed.

NINE

Family of Light Blessing

Another client named Neli was taken to meet several groups of intelligent beings who are supporting this grand transition.

C: I feel more like a spirit. Like an energy spirit, like a round energy. Yeah, I travel all over. It feels like that. I travel all over if I want to. There are no colors, more transparent. A bright light. Feel safe but still, there is a concern about Earth. Like I am picking up information from Mother Earth. That's the concern. I am receiving information that all is not well. Something has shifted. This energy is coming in, this dark energy. It was not there before. It's like it's moving in from the sky. Like a big storm coming in, but it's not a storm; it's energy. It's dark, and it feels like sticky energy.

NEXT SCENE: JESUS BRINGS THE LIGHT

C: I feel that I am standing on the Earth right now, and I can see all of the rainbow colors. I see Jesus. He's telling me that all is well. That he has come to lift the darkness. And I see him walking the Earth like his footsteps are prints on the Earth. There are some birds flying in the sky. It's showing he takes long walks alone. He can change everything in an instant. It may seem like a long walk, but it can change immediately.

M: When you say it changes, what do you mean?

C: I don't know. I see him dividing the sea. He caught the fish. Miracles.

M: What kind of miracles?

C: Like dividing the fish and dividing the sea and changing the scenery. He's telling us now that we can all do this in this lifetime. We can do this ourselves. That we can welcome this right now, we can welcome change. We have to believe in it. We have to believe that we can. He walked the Earth to show us. He is giving it to us now. It's up to us now.

M: Like he's passing a torch?

C: Yeah. It's time to change gears. It's time.

M: I wonder what he means by it's time to change gears.

C: *We have all the answers inside of us. We need to believe it. We need to believe that all is possible; there are so many still going on in our old beliefs. We have new paths to walk now; we have new dimensions to walk. He will walk with us. He wants to walk with us. He has come to do so now with all the humans that are ready to walk with him. He is walking with everyone ready to do so. He's with us. So much, so much. He's here because it's time to take the next step.*

M: I wonder what the next step is.

C: *It's to act in PURPOSE. To ACT at the next level. To let go of the physicality in the way we believe in it. To understand that everything is energy. It's not what it seems like. The lightworkers are ready now. We have this deep, deep, deep information inside of all of us that is available. It wants to come through us, but we have to go inside. We will never find it on the outside. We find it on the inside out. The deep information it's like soul-level type of information. We have discernment of what we are to give. We have to stay true to ourselves, to our path, to our truth. Nothing but the truth. We all have a flame in our hearts. It has a lot of information; it will show us the way. We need to go inside. When it opens, we go through a new passage. To know ourselves. The grand awakening. We are ready now. We are so ready.*

M: How does one go into their heart? How do they unlock it?

C: *There are different ways. Every person is to find their way. What makes them feel good. To be romanced. To turn down the volume of the outside and unlock the inside. The best way to do that for yourself is to sit in meditation. For some, it's to take a walk in nature. It takes you into the space where you feel expanded. It's easier now because every step we take, where we are right now, it's going to be easier. I get a picture of the darkness moving into Earth, inside of Earth to the middle part within the Earth; it's also the same picture for us. The darkness has moved further inside.*

M: What does that mean?

C: *It means it's ready to be released. It needs to be released from the inside, from the inner Light, from the inner realms of Light — where we have lots of lots of lots of Light helping. The darkness can come to light.*

M: So, these light beings are helping to clear this dark energy?

C: *Yeah, if we turn inward. If we don't turn inward, it will have to play out in the outer.*

M: So, the more of us that go inward, the more the energy gets cleared?

C: Wow, yes. It will affect the whole Earth. The whole consciousness of Earth.

M: What happens if we don't go inward. What happens?

C: It will continue to play out the way it used to. We will see a lot of darkness playing out because it's the only way it can be seen. When it's seen, there is a chance for it to transmute into awareness. The faster way is to go inside and ask for the help. I see it's complex; it's like thousands and thousands and thousands of light beings and angels inside. They're just waiting for us to cross over. They're like, "Come on, let's go through this portal so we can receive you, so we can welcome you home." They are so ready to welcome us home. They have waited so long for this.

M: So, this going inward is the way to them?

C: It's the only way.

M: I wonder if they can give us a process of going in so we can connect with them and make the change.

C: It's about being still, not letting your world deceive you or lead you outside to yourself. To practice stillness and to almost see like a lantern inside that grows bigger and bigger. It's like a feeling. The feel of soft alignment. It's not difficult; we are not looking for big things.

SCENE: MESSAGE FROM MARY

C: Mary. I see her. She is so beautiful, giving the divine spark of the divine feminine. She is giving it to us. To humanity. To us all. She is surrounding the Earth with it. She is also in each individual heart. She's holding this soft light like she's showing the way into the heart — the path of softening yourself. To not have expectations. It's like walking through the door, and Mary is on the other side. So close, to be kind to yourself. To be at peace with yourself. To not make life so difficult. To feel like you can always turn inward to the softness because she is waiting there with her soft light taking you through. They are all there taking us through. They are all helping, but Jesus and Mary are coming through because we know them so well.

M: So, because we have more of a collective relationship with them, they are more at the forefront?

C: Yeah. It makes it easier for us.

M: But there is help coming from many?

C: Oh, there are so many.

NEXT SCENE: MESSAGES FROM INNER EARTH

C: Showing a lot of people under the Earth. There are many under the crust of the Earth. They are blue beings. They are here to help us love. They are coming, more and more, to the surface, but we are not quite ready.

M: Do they have anything to share?

C: They will when the time is ready. It's not right now. We need to go through this portal. When we do, they will be available but also help us pass through. It's not time now to be heard. They want us to know they are there.

M: I am wondering, what needs to happen for people to go through this portal? I know many are doing heart-based practices and connecting with their heart. What needs to happen for someone to make the transition?

C: It's on a collective scale. We know about the frustration you must feel that you are working hard to make the passage, but it's more like a tipping point. And it's very, very close to that tipping point right now and that's why we say it has become easier to go inside this portal because when many people do it at the same time, when we practice this all together, it will take over. It will be easier and easier. The tipping point is like being in a new place. Everything will change from the inside out. That's what we are waiting for right now.

M: What are some ways we can accelerate this process?

C: It's this softness. More feminine space. Softness. To allow. Not to run after things, not to try to make it happen, it's more like a process of leaning inwards softly like a soft, warm embrace of ourselves. We don't have to work as much as we used to do. We don't have to work as much on clearing, on clearing our bodies, because it's happening all the time. So, we can drop these exercises more and more and just be. Be the feeling. Be in the center. Take your place in the center of your being. Practice alignment. And then, at the same time, it's a waiting process until the tipping point is reached. The tipping point will happen. It may feel like you are doing too little, but sometimes that is better than doing a lot or doing in general. Everyone can come into a softer focus, and when we allow, things will come to us.

NEXT SCENE: MESSAGES FROM STAR FAMILY

C: (Laughs) Hmm. Oh. I see (laughs) extraterrestrials. They look like small beings, but they have such fun energy. They are stamping and clapping. I see them as a group consciousness.

M: Do they have anything they want to share?

C: They want to share joy! Joy, joy, joy! Lots of joy! They want to lift us into the new with joy. They are sending us the joy — upliftment. It's uplifting energy. Ah, what they are doing — clapping and stamping — they are doing it to raise the vibration. It's actually time to celebrate. It's right around the corner. They are already celebrating. It's so close, and we have come through the darkness, even with what we see play out — it's in the past. It just shows because people are holding it in their perception. It's really in the past.

M: What about when things...I'll give an example that is coming from American culture right now. It's being presented to the whole world how women were hurt in the past and so this is bringing up a strong charge from all the other women who have been hurt by men, by different situations, and I am seeing people grab onto it, attached to that story. How can we individually and collectively work with things like that? That have a charge to it? That have a history of being hurt?

C: It's meant to play out. It's part of the collective. It's part of Earth's memories. Earth is releasing these memories, and of course, every human being is connected to Earth, so it's like an earthquake inside of these human beings. The best way to go about it is to be in love, connectedness, awareness, to embrace and help each other to embrace it. To move in from a high vibration, if possible, to create a high vibration in order to caress it. To envelop it. It needs to be freed; it needs to have its outpouring. It's needed. A deep cry, a deep sense of hurt, it needs to come through, but see it only as the past and not to hang onto it too much. Not have too many stories around it, don't give it too much attention. It's guided to come through.

M: Beautiful. What else are you seeing now?

C: I see the Earth is opening up.

M: What do you see?

C: I see two Earths. And then I see many, many Earths. There are as many Earths as humans. It means that every human has its own individual Earth experience.

M: Beautiful, what happens next?

C: It's the same energy coming through for us; it's the same for us. Our heart energy is the same. The One is returning to us.

M: The same flame in our hearts is in the center of the Earth?

C: Yeah, but also the humans. Every heart is the same material, the same energy, the same One. The same Creator.

M: The energy of the One is in all of us.

C: Yes, and in the center of the Earth as well. In all the Earths. It's time to come together as One.

Closing Statement

I hope that this material has activated multidimensional awakening and expansion for you. I hope that it brings you comfort and joy as we make our way through this transitionary corridor between old Earth and the New Earth. May you count your blessings and walk your path with increasing faith and luminous devotion. The best is yet to come!

Now, let us make our way into the PATH OF AWAKENING: KEYS FOR TRANSFIGURATION material!

TEN

Ascension Symptom Care

Lightbody ascension practices are found in many ancient cultures, especially in India, Tibet, and Ancient Egypt. The systems focus on transformation by refining the physical, vital, emotional, mental, intuitional, intellectual, and spiritual bodies so that a being embodies Divine Light and their Divine I AM Presence. As we clear our lower energies, we make way for the Light of the Higher Realms to descend into our physical vessel so that we radiate Light and Truth out into the world.

In the past, once an initiate reached a high enough vibration and the highest level of enlightenment they could reach in the body, they would consciously shed the body to continue learning in the higher realms in their Lightbody. Sometimes they would go into a trance and consciously leave the body, or some highly advanced initiates who could control the frequency of their cells would spin them faster and faster until they shifted beyond the visible light spectrum into the higher realms as their physical body dissolved into thin air. Yeshua ben Joseph (Jesus) made this ascension process popular, but it has also been documented and written about by other cultures, especially the Egyptians and Tibetan Buddhists.

What is different about our upcoming ascension is that we will be transforming our physical body into a lighter form and taking it with us into the next dimension of consciousness and reality. What was once only available to select initiates through arduous purification and healing practices in secluded temples and monasteries is now available to all people committed to compassionate heart-based living and have done the work to raise their overall vibration.

As we prepare for Gaia's transformation from Third Density Earth to Fourth Density Gaia, our DNA is being restored back to the Adamic form, the original pristine human Lightbody. Many alterations have been made to the human DNA throughout humanity's time on Earth, and we are in a purging process of all the distortions stored within our multidimensional genetic structure and sequencing.

These distortions are the product of genetic implantation from other star races, ancestral memory, mental fields absorbed from the collective thought patterns, toxicity from our environments, damage from the cataclysm of Atlantis, and more. As these ascension energies move through our system, they clear any blockages we have accrued so that we can hold more light. This can appear as cold/flu-like symptoms, increased body heat, heightened intuition, foggy mind, dizziness, chest pain, digestive issues, vivid dreams, emotional purging, paranormal experiences, ringing in the ears, dehydration, and more.

Below is a list of guidelines to support the ascension and Lightbody activation and recalibration processes. This is not meant to be "medical advice" but speaks to common experiences held by myself and others in the global ascension community.

If you feel that you are unhealthy and at risk for serious health concerns, please see a medical professional. I highly recommend seeing a medical professional who treats clients holistically. Western medicine is trained to focus on symptoms. Eastern medicine and holistic healthcare professionals are trained to look for root causes and treat entire systems to bring the body back into homeostasis.

Meditation: Calling in Light

Meditation is a crucial step in this process. Developing self-awareness helps you discern what is best for your path so that you can release what no longer serves you. Meditation practices that utilize conscious breathing are some of the best tools to ground your energy, clear out stagnant energy, and revitalize your personal energy field as fresh life force enters through the breath. Visualizing clear, bright light moving through the body helps raise the body's vibration and transform dense energy into a more refined and clear energy signature. Let the sunshine in!

Dehydration

Many health problems stem from chronic dehydration. Drink plenty of fresh spring water to hydrate the tissues and cells of the body. Municipal water sources often contain chlorine, fluoride, or other chemicals that poison our bodies and mind. Adding trace-mineral hydration salts to your water helps the water absorb into the cells. Also, consider taking a "cell salt" supplement to support healthy cellular function. Adding magnesium to your hydration practice will also help with discomfort in the chest/heart region when assimilating the energies. This will also help with headaches and anxious feelings.

Silica Supplements

It has been recommended that we all take silica supplements to support our body's transition from being carbon-based to a crystalline, silica-based Lightbody. This will help with achy joints, cognitive functioning, and more.

Essential Oils and Plant Medicine

Nature knows best. Herbs and plant extracts work with our body's cells and consciousness to bring our systems into homeostasis. This includes medicines like psylocibin, cannabis, hemp, kava, and other plant allies to help us soothe the ascension process and connect with higher intelligence for healing and transformation. Of course, intention and safety are important for all medicine journeys. Keep it sacred!

High-quality essential oils that are certified pure and organic safely work with the body's cells to support the body's natural ability to heal itself. Some oils can be taken internally, and most are safe for topical and aromatic use. Check with each oil's health and protocol guidelines to understand how to use the oil safely and properly.

When using topically, consider using a vegetable/nut-based carrier oil to help spread the essential oil across the skin. If an essential oil is applied topically and causes irritation, dilute and clean with a carrier oil. Do not use water as this drives the essential oil further into the tissue.

Detoxify the Body

Physical symptoms include a variety of detoxification symptoms as toxins are released from the body. You may notice a diet change as the body craves fresh, organic fruits and vegetables and less meat. There will not be meat or killing of any kind when we shift to the New Earth consciousness.

Everyone should follow their own guidance about what nourishment their body needs at any given time. Periodic fasting can help the elimination process as well as eating a naturally detoxifying diet. Eating fresh greens fills the body systems with biophotons, light particles to support healthy system functionality. Switch to natural, organic products versus products with toxic chemical ingredients to reduce your organs' toxic load. You may feel guided to do a cleanse regimen like a liver cleanse or kidney cleanse, or a heavy metal detox to help the body eliminate toxins.

Cellular Oxidation

Radiation from cosmic energies, solar events, 5G radiation, and other energies puts stress on our body's cells. Increase antioxidant intake and supplements that promote cellular health and reverse the effects of oxidative stress.

Alkalize the Body

Reduce the body's acidity to reduce inflammation and support the body's natural ability to heal itself. This includes eating a mostly "sattvic" diet or a "yogic diet" which is simple and free from processed ingredients and synthetics. Practices like drinking apple cider vinegar, fresh lemon juice, or citrus essential oils help to break apart and eliminate toxic build-up in the body.

Detoxify People, Places, and Things

Spend less and less time around people that are vexatious to your system. Find like-minded people who are loving and gentle to spend your time with. Avoid places with highly charged energies when you are feeling extra sensitive. Many find that they need to spend more quality time alone or with their pets and limit their social interactions to focus on their own healing and expansion. Declutter your home to free up stagnant energy. As within, so without!

Rest and Sleep

Listen to the body and honor when it is asking for rest. At times, the body will need much more rest and sleep as it adjusts to the shifting frequencies. Sometimes, you may not be able to sleep because of the rush of plasma entering your field from the ascension energies. Be gentle with yourself. Natural sleep aids, teas, and herbal supplements help the body stay in deeper sleep to feel refreshed when you awaken. Chamomile and lavender can help you prepare for a deep night's rest.

Get Into Nature

Nature has a grounding and centering effect on our consciousness and nervous system. Take frequent trips into nature away from people, pollution, and technology. "Earthing" or walking barefoot on the ground helps to ground pent-up energy in your nervous system, leaving you feeling grounded and clear. If you cannot stand on soil, you can stand on a layer of sea salt to ground your energy. Use a container to stand in so that you do not make a mess!

Ringing in the Ears

The electromagnetic fields of the Earth and the planetary grid will be unstable in the process, as will our own energetic field. The ringing of the ears is common for people at different times as waves of plasma enter the Earth. Some people find themselves to be extra sensitive to Electromagnetic Frequencies (EMFs). Many devices and crystals (e.g., shungite) are available to help reduce the negative effects of EMFs on the body and consciousness. It is suggested that we take as much time as we can to get off our devices, out of range of Wi-Fi and cell towers, and immerse ourselves in the regenerative field of Nature. Return to the wild and wonderful!

Headaches, Dizziness, and Cognitive Functioning

These energies affect our minds as we shed lower beliefs and upgrade the brain's anatomy and cognitive functioning. This could manifest as states of confusion and feeling sensations in the brain, including headaches, energy movement, and pulsations.

Dizziness and headaches can be a sign that you need more water and need to ground excess energy. Consciously ground the energy through intention and meditative practices or walk barefoot on the earth. Increase water intake and rest until the dizziness subsides. Add hydration salts, trace minerals, cellular salts, and silica supplements to support the process. Essential oils like peppermint and lavender help soothe head and neck tension to alleviate pressure in the head.

Digestive System Issues

The digestive system not only processes food to create energy, but the solar plexus digests subtle energy for a variety of processes. Many find that their digestive system is either over or underactive at different times. I recommend using a natural digestive supplement, digestive enzyme supplement, or laying of hands to support the healing process. Essential oils like ginger and peppermint help support healthy digestive processes.

Low Energy and Fatigue

Sometimes, no matter how much you rest, it may not feel like enough. Using invigorating essential oils can boost the mood and increase focus. There are many natural food supplements to use to boost energy like cacao, maca, and spirulina. If you use caffeine, I suggest using tea, especially yerba mate, versus coffee to reduce acidity in the body. Essential oils like peppermint and citrus oils help to lift the mood and focus the mind.

Soaking in Water

Water is a powerful tool to use to ground and clear energy. Find natural sources of water to swim in or soak your feet. Take baths with natural salts and minerals added to the water to help clear and restore. Adding your favorite essential oils, candles, and soft music or recorded meditations helps amplify the bath's healing effects. Frequent showers also help to reinvigorate the senses and clear your personal energy.

Emotional Triggering and Heart Activation

Collective, ancestral, and individual trauma stored within the body's systems and DNA are being reactivated and cleared. Many experience this as a deep churning in the heart, fatigue, vivid dreams, and more. Aromatherapy is one of the quickest natural ways to soothe emotions.

Increased Intuitive Abilities

Intuition, psychic gifts, and multidimensional awareness are increasing rapidly as our lower energies clear out of the chakra and subtle energy systems, creating an expanded empathetic nervous system. To avoid unnecessary suffering and psychic attack, one can cultivate a strong and clear subtle energy system and grow in heart-centered discernment and energetic hygiene.

Vivid and Prophetic Dreams

Many are experiencing vivid dreams as their subconscious works out limiting beliefs and unprocessed trauma in their dreamtime. Some dreams are teaching dreams where people experience themselves in learning environments practicing new skills. Some are healing dreams where people report miraculous, rapid healing often conducted by extraterrestrial beings or higher light beings. Some people are reporting meetings with other souls in their soul group, where Ascension topics are discussed. Some people are reporting that they are being brought aboard spacecraft and introduced to galactic beings and receive updated intel on Earth changes and Ascension information.

Some people do not have any dream recall during the ascension process because the information being discussed in the dreams would keep them from playing out the role they need to in their regular human life. Some people have even traveled to the New Earth or future timelines where they get to experience life after humanity and Earth have ascended.

Each person is different in how they handle this process. Do not judge yourself based on how others are handling it. Also, one minute you can be fine, and the next minute have an emotional purge and a headache. Let the process happen. Make a practice of nourishing yourself.

This process can be intense, but it comes with great benefits! Thank you for facing your shadow and aligning with Truth, Knowledge, and Wisdom. You are so brave!

ELEVEN

Shifting to New Earth

We are now at the final moments before this Grand Shift. From a higher perspective, we are being divided between positive polarity collectives and negative polarity collectives. This means that some are awakening to a higher love within, and others are maintaining a duality-based consciousness and will continue a downward spiral of entropy and destruction, eventually exiting the planet through physical death.

Over the coming years, people will be moving on the planet to the places they have decided to be for these final events leading up to the Main Event Horizon and shift in consciousness. Those who are awakening are beginning to find others who are awakening. Much of this has been happening on the internet, and more and more events and gatherings will be happening across the world as people come together in One Heart. What a cause for celebration as we all begin to see the familiar Light in one another's eyes and awaken to the game we have been playing with ourselves since the beginning of time.

Not everyone is meant to continue with Earth and ascending humanity into this next Age of Light. Their souls will continue their maturation process in other incarnations on other planets where the Third Dimension exists or whatever dimension best serves their growth. Some of these embodied souls are seen as the "villains" and "traitors" that will catalyze and amplify the desire to awaken in the hearts and minds of those who are choosing Love, Light, Unity, and Harmony. The villain archetype is crucial for Ascension. We see this character in Set from Egypt for the resurrection of Osiris and in Judas for the ascension process of Jesus. Each awakening soul is invited to play the role of Collective Messiahship and share the good news of Ascension and the Higher Mysteries so that those who hunger for Truth can be set free from the entropic thought patterns of service-to-self, ancestral trauma, and negative karma.

It is wise to remember that "everything is not what it seems" in this school of illusion. Everything is happening for a Divine Purpose. We are invited to stand as pillars of Unconditional Love and broadcast the messages of New Earth. For those who have ears to listen, let them hear the "good news" of what is to come. Let us all reveal the thought processes and beliefs that have created our own inner tyrant and an inner adversary so that we no longer need to see it outpictured in our reality. Let us choose peace. Let us choose harmony. Let us choose unity. Let us choose Ascension!

Prophecy

Anyone who does intuitive readings can tell you that their prophecies and intuitive understandings are based on energy at that particular moment of the vision or reading. Free will gives us the ability to choose a higher timeline by releasing density and making higher choices. With so many volunteers and support from galactic beings and the higher realms, we have moved beyond much of the death and destruction that has been foretold by prophets and seers of the past. Even modern prophecies are subject to change as we are constantly shifting between probabilities of how this will all play out.

Every action you as an individual or we as a collective make shifts us into different timeline potentials for the unfolding of The Event. Our job is to maintain the highest vibration and the highest vision for the highest potential outcome so that we can guide our collective experience into a more harmonious unfolding. The power is in our hands, minds, and hearts. We can come together as a collective and use the power of focused attention and loving intention to guide us all into peace and unity. The power and potency of positive and empowering prayer holds the keys to manifesting our most desired outcomes. While some cataclysmic events are necessary for this shift to occur, we can avoid unnecessary suffering by coming together in unified prayer. Together, we can create a powerful prayer field to influence weather patterns, seismic activity, and harmonize collective emotional experiences to avoid events that could cause massive suffering and transition to a higher timeline of experience.

There will be those that will stay focused on the doom and gloom narrative that is widely accepted and propagated by world religions. By focusing on the darkness and suffering, they will likely create that experience for themselves on their personal timeline. We, as the human collective, do have the ability to collapse timelines that no longer serve us. We have a choice. It is the same choice that there has always been — between unconditional love and surrender to the Divine Plan or else live in fear, judgment, and inner turmoil. Even when chaotic events are happening around the world, it is up to us to hold the highest outcome in our vision and be unwavering in our ability to hold the Light.

Discernment and False Teachers

Discernment is of the utmost importance at this time. When the energies are high, so are the emotions. Many wild and misleading ideas will be shared amongst the collective. It is up to each individual to grow in the power of discernment to feel what resonates as Truth within them. If a message generates fear or panic within you, walk away from that material. Many religious leaders, government officials, and spiritual teachers will have their shadows brought into the light where they have abused their power, especially those who have claimed to be the voice of God. This includes the ascension community! It is important not to put any human on a pedestal. We are all subject to shadow. Instead, place your faith in your Inner Light and the unfolding of the higher evolutionary plan. For the most part, I have stopped listening to most spiritual teachers and have instead invested time learning to listen to my own internal guidance and the study of sacred texts to grow in my own spiritual capacity. Follow your heart. It knows the way. The mechanics of discernment are taught later in this book in the section about the *vijnanamaya kosha*, the Intellectual Wisdom Body.

Many Are Exiting the Earth School

Once a soul has aligned with an exit plan, no outside force can stop it from exiting. Many people will leave their bodies during these events per their design before entering this life. Every contract has to play out, and a balance must be achieved. As these souls go through their physical death experience, they will support us from the "other side." Another reason people die is that they take their fear and karma out of the Earth realm, which increases the collective vibration of Earth.

As the shadow systems and shadow players are revealed to the masses, many will have to face the fact that they have supported these systems unknowingly and in doing so have supported systems that have killed countless people. I was told that when the truth comes out about the cancer industry, many will be outraged because of all the loved ones they lost from cancer and other illnesses that could have been saved if the controllers had not created the conditions that cause cancer and repressed the healing technologies and medicines. Many people will have to face the fact that they ridiculed us "new agers" and "conspiracy theorists" who were right all along. Disclosure of the shadow system will cause people to have heart attacks from a broken heart; people will kill one another in rage; many will commit suicide or die from psychosis because they cannot live with the truth.

Some people will not be able to hold the vibration of these high energies and die suddenly or quickly decline in health because they have not shed dense energies and will not evolve. Some souls decided they would leave the Earth School as a group, possibly in a natural disaster or casualty of violence. During these times, we will need one another to support each other through the natural grieving processes. This is another reason why we need more people with a higher perspective of death and the afterlife, as many will be looking for answers.

Not everyone is meant to ascend into the New Earth. Some are meant to have simple lives and exit this world for the next journey throughout the cosmos. Ascension involves reconciling judgment within us for those who seem not to be "waking up" or seem to be following the false narrative presented by the controllers. They are offering us an opportunity to release polarized perspectives and be open to nondual understanding. Even the most "evil" people are offering us bitter medicine to grow into deeper compassion and clarity. This does not mean that we condone the actions that cause harm, it just means that we do not have to hold hatred, judgment, or contempt towards them. Every single being here on the planet is serving this great awakening whether they are conscious of it or not. All is Source; all is the One Being experiencing itself in myriad forms and polarities for the purpose of truly "knowing thy Self."

Much grief will sweep through humanity during these next stages. They are the most difficult to bear and many will experience intense grief. Grief is a powerful emotion. It carves deep into the heart and seems to stay around for eternity for some. We can use the power of High Alchemy to use grief as a powerful tool for transformation. I invite us all to use the pain of what is to come to launch us into our sovereign power to reform our reality. Use it to become a voice for the Earth and for those who have suffered under the tyranny of these shadow systems. All of this ends when humanity stands in its power and says ENOUGH!

Rapture

This is a complex multidimensional topic because I have only heard of this a few times. This type of event is not connected to any religion. Since it is a common question, I will share what I have learned through my sessions.

The first point to share is that there will not be a mass disappearance of bodies as depicted in some modern Christian interpretations. The main way of departure will be from people leaving their bodies through physical death as they finish their contracts. This is not a judgment. It is simply part of the plan as they have only agreed to live through so much of the process.

One other type of departure I have heard of, but only once, is the departure of some starseeds. I have heard of two major departures from the planet for souls from other star systems who volunteered to incarnate on Earth as humans to assist in the Great Awakening. Some starseeds are only on the planet to help energetically until a tipping point occurs in our collective consciousness. Once that marker is reached, one large group of people will be taken from the planet, followed by another group a few months later. I have been told that there are twelve "New Earths" including this one that we are all currently on. Each of these planets will be home to different humans and life forms. I do not know much about the other planets as much of my sessions have been focused on the shift of Gaia/Terra from the Third Density to the Fourth, aka the Fifth Dimension. From my understanding, there will be considerably fewer people living on the planet once it finalizes its shift.

In my second meeting with the Council of 24 Elders, I was shown how I would have the capacity to jump between realities or embodiments. It seemed as though I would be able to be in one embodiment in 5D New Earth and then "flip myself inside out" to be in the 3D Earth reality to assist in some way as if I would be living in both realities simultaneously. I still do not completely understand what was shown to me, but I thought I would write about it in case it is helpful for someone. Part of the intention with this book is to have the book printed in physical form so that it would be available for people if timelines split into different experiences of The Event.

It is common for people to question if they are going to "make it." This question is rooted in fear and insecurity and deserves time for reflection and healing so that you can embody the higher love of your Divine Nature. No one is "left behind" which means that you are exactly where you need to be, and Source is with you always. Trust in the process and stay present in your heart.

Potential Timelines of War

As part of the design, service-to-self forces will likely destroy one another as they war against each other to control the planet. War, battles, protests, revolts, riots, and other such events are likely to happen as we get closer to the launch point of the main event — the pulse of Light from our Sun via the Great Central Sun.

This experience of war is for those who agreed to such an experience before incarnating. There will be places of peace and places of conflict. Those who exit the Earth School are simply done with their life contract and will continue to their next incarnation in whatever level of spiritual growth is appropriate for them. The wars and destruction serve as a contrast for those who are awakening to anchor us into knowing that Love and Peace are truly The Way.

True and lasting peace, the Heaven on Earth reality is not possible in the third dimension. This true peace and harmony are found in the fifth-dimensional consciousness. Until then, conflict and duality remain as karmic contracts play out before 5D consciousness fully manifests across the remnant of humanity upon 5D Earth.

My understanding is that there are a few different groups of service-to-self consciousness that are fighting for control of the planet and humanity. The overlord structures coordinate events to create a crisis and suffering and then offer a solution to manipulate people to follow their agenda (problem-reaction-solution). This bait-and-hook method of mind control hijacks the goodwill intentions and actions of the unaware who unknowingly follow the mainstream narrative because they feel that they are helping the situation. Coordinated power outages, food and supply shortages, and other false flag events are planned to create fear in humanity. Those who are connected to their inner truth and higher consciousness connection will be able to see these events for what they truly are, while others will not as they are still under the spell.

This dark initiative is powered through psychological manipulation tactics used through subliminal messaging and suggestion using the trance-induced state created by watching a television or screened device. Phrases are repeated by global leaders, politicians, and other influential people to implant the overlord-approved narrative into the listeners' consciousness which subconsciously programs them to follow the nefarious agenda. The war on consciousness and the battle for dominion over Planet Earth and humanity is real and we are watching it play out in real time.

Collapsing of the Old Systems

All of society's systems are being forced to shift with this energy or crumble to make way for the new. Governments, financial institutions, religious institutions, judicial systems, educational systems, and so on have been used to keep humanity in the lower consciousness and enslaved through various methods. All of these systems will be reconciled over the next years. This is especially true of the collapse of the financial systems which must dissolve so that the Cabal-run control systems that depend on currency to fund their dark projects will run out of financial backing. Humanity will no longer "chase the dollar" to create their worth or security and will instead realize their inherent worth and source all that they need from the quantum field and Gaia.

Governing systems will shift towards councils of representatives who will be selected based on spiritual resonance. In the New Earth, everyone will perform the role that is most in alignment with their soul's path. No more slave jobs! The old system of economics will give way to a quantum-based financial system.

Earth Changes

Parallel to our ascension symptoms, Gaia is going through her own clearing process before she shifts into her higher, lighter form. Volunteers on the surface and galactic beings have been assisting this transition by helping Gaia transmute some of the dense energy built up over millions of years. Seismic and volcanic activity, massive storms, and abnormal weather patterns are likely to increase as the planet's energies and toxic areas are cleansed. This is like a cat or a dog that shakes and shimmies after it gets injured. This natural movement is mirrored by the Earth as Gaia releases her pent-up energy.

Gaia is a powerful and sovereign being. She permits humanity to live upon her and go through the karmic lessons necessary to remember our higher consciousness identity and unity with All. What we see happening with the Earth in terms of climate change is a reflection of the imbalance within us. She is incredibly patient with us. She could shake us all off in a heartbeat if she wanted to! The Controllers have been using the "save the Earth" narrative to convince us to give up our freedoms and to pay more money to fill their bank accounts. If we truly want the Earth to be clean and clear, it is the global elite control systems that need to be dissolved so that the land can be freed up. It is the greed born from service-to-self consciousness that needs to be eradicated. I imagine that the Controllers will use the Earth changes to further their narrative but those who know, who are connected to Spirit and our Earth Mother, will know what is truly occurring.

Crustal shifts, pole shifts, and water displacement will reorient the planet's surface as has happened in previous resets (Lemuria and Atlantis). This will reveal lost temples, lost technologies, and lost artifacts that will remind humanity of its galactic legacy. I was told that the Galactic Federation is working with the tectonic plates to balance the plasma of the core of the Earth to open up telepathic communication with Inner Earth civilizations such as Telos, Agartha, and other civilizations who have been keeping ancient records and protecting advanced technologies from the times of Lemuria and Atlantis specifically for these times. While many humans have already been communicating with Inner Earth beings, physical meetings will begin soon.

I have heard of many big fires around the world as well. I share this information cautiously because I know that we can create the future that we want. It all comes down to the collective consciousness intention and what we have agreed to in our soul contracts before incarnating. Again, I have been told that much of the destruction has been averted already and that Earth changes will not be as severe as once prophesied.

This is a natural process, and there is nothing to fear. You are always where you need to be. If you feel safe, you are safe. If you follow fear, you have the potential to create that outcome. It is up to us to become aware of our fearful tendencies and refine them through Higher Knowledge and Faith. Trust that you are being guided to the right place for the right timing of these events.

It is wise to have some supplies available if power outages or other events occur. Having a few weeks' worth of food, water, and basic supplies can be useful if supply chains are cut off because of these shifts and changes. There are potentials for communication systems and power supplies to go down at different stages. I am told that around this time awakened people will have developed a level of telepathy that will help us communicate without the need for these systems. I am told the Earth changes will begin after the big disclosures have started and sometime after the "illusion of food shortages" and power and communication system failures created by the Cabal. One sign to watch for is the birds. I imagine that before the major Earth changes start, the migratory pathways will be disrupted for birds and other animals like whales and fish who use the electromagnetic pathways to navigate across the Earth.

Safe Havens and New Earth Communities

During this Grand Shift into the next era, safe havens will need to be organized while society goes through its transformation. Some clients speak about schools and centers of education where people will gather soon while various events and changes are happening worldwide. The centers will be high-vibrational environments where people can heal, connect with one another, and support others as people continue to be drawn to these vortexes. We have heard mostly about the first City of Light that will be developed in the Pacific Northwest. This community will be a place for us to create a reality that is "off to the side" from the chaos of the crumbling world. I am not sure exactly how it starts to be manifested, but I have heard that eventually this higher dimensional, etheric, crystalline city that many starseeds see in dreams and meditation will be anchored to the Earth realm. The fires in that region are clearing out the old templates held by the land and the people that need to be released to make room for the new. Many of us have this shared dream of living in healing communities because we designed this plan before we came into the Earth School. Ron and I are excited to be a part of catalyzing that collective dream and manifesting this New Earth community.

Experimental Injections

The rollout and use of the inoculations for Covid-19 are playing a significant part in the Ascension. It is an introduction of a major catalyst that will mean different things for every person, every family, every nation, and the collective story of humanity. Each of us has a unique path, and they are all part of the divine coordination of this ascension event.

In the Bible, the "End Times" prophecy speaks of the "Mark of the Beast" being implemented to control humanity. According to the prophecy, those who do not have the mark would not be able to buy or sell. This control structure sounds remarkably similar to what is happening with the inoculations for Covid-19 and the planned "Vaccine Passports" beginning to be implemented by different governments around the world. While some of the world believes the mainstream media narrative, many see this as an attempt by those in service-to-self consciousness to control and manipulate humanity. Hopefully such an experience of tyrannical control never comes to full manifestation.

The information coming through many quantum healing hypnosis sessions is that these inoculations will negatively affect the health of many people and the worldwide push for vaccination is intended to initiate humanity into another level of overlord control, moving us towards a one world tyrannical government structure. While all of the vaccines will cause issues globally, the bigger issue has to do with the negative fallout from the mRNA gene therapies. At the writing of this book, there are already global reports of myocarditis, pericarditis, rapidly growing aggressive cancers, pulmonary embolism, and sudden death. Anyone who speaks out against the Covid-19 narrative is censored, deplatformed, or silenced. I have a feeling we are just beginning to see the tip of the iceberg in terms of the long-term effects of these injections.

In my sessions, it has been described how the service-to-self forces are using the injections to broadcast low-frequency thought patterning into the injected people, causing a distortion in their minds that lowers their vibration. Something in the injections also connects the injected person to a massive Artificial Intelligence network that extends beyond this planet that tracks the people who have been injected. The signal strength of the AI technology weakens at around six months which is part of the reason for additional booster shots. It was shared that individuals have the ability to recode the AI technology and use it to broadcast light frequencies back into the AI network to assist in the dismantling of that system.

Just because someone took an injection does not necessarily mean they cannot ascend or will get sick. The human body can transmute ANYTHING! That is part of the magnificence of human design. We can overcome every entropic pattern and transform it into the highest light. Although, I certainly would not want to test that capacity on myself! Every time I have asked, there is not yet a technology on the Earth that can reverse the negative fallout, but many physical and subtle body detoxification protocols are being downloaded by lightworkers to assist in detoxification and repair. We have been told that the IQH sessions will assist with this in the future.

It is necessary to have a high light quotient and be in outstanding health and cohesion to transmute this negative technology. Detoxification protocols should be followed for the physical and subtle bodies to clear out the negative components of the injections. The people who have taken these injections must hold no resistance to the divine and clear their various bodies with whatever means necessary. If you have taken the inoculations and wish to clear them from your system, I want you to know that I believe in you and your capacity to turn this situation into something that feeds your spiritual growth and catalyzes your process of liberation. We are here to assist!

Many people have turned from the Love of Source and do not take good care of their bodies and have not awakened to the higher Light. They are going to have the most difficult job transmuting the negative effects of the inoculations and many will leave the planet.

For some people, taking the inoculation is a sign that they are still hypnotized by the narrative that is being pushed on them by the Controllers and are unawakened or just in the beginning stages of awakening. Some will take the inoculation because they have meditated on it and fully trust that this is part of their divine pathway. They are not doing it from lower ego reasons but because of divine guidance. Some will not choose to take the injections because they prefer the organic immunity of the human body and do not want to take any risk.

Now we are at the waiting and witnessing stage as we watch what these inoculations do to humanity. For some, it will be part of their exit plan from the Earth School. As I said, not everyone is meant to ascend. Some are meant to have simple lives and transition out. Many will be born in new bodies on New Earth or continue in other schools. For some, it will be a catalyst for major awakening. For planet Earth, it begins the crumbling of the "sick-for-profit" system and the rising of the people against the forces of darkness and control.

The hardest part for those taking and not taking is not to judge or go into states of fear. Even the inoculations are a test to see if we follow the *maya* into the suffering mind or if we stay in loving conscious awareness. This does not mean that we should not speak out against tyranny and injustice, yet we can let our voices be heard from a place of true empowerment and nonviolence. One who is united with their True Nature is more powerful than one thousand who are not. Together, we ARE THE WINDS OF CHANGE!

Another challenge is that during this bifurcation of consciousness, the Great Divide, most of the people that have taken the inoculations are in a different consciousness that will be difficult for ascension-focused people to be around. Our reality may be offensive to them because we are not under the spell of the mainstream narrative. It is a two-world split. We live in completely different realities side by side. The Old Earth consciousness and the New Earth consciousness occupy the Earth at the same time. I suggest finding your people, those with the Light in their eyes! Those who are on the path of seeking spiritual wisdom and spiritual knowledge. These are the ones you will build the New Earth with!

Artificial Intelligence and Microchip Implants

It is wise to exercise extreme caution when creating Artificial Intelligence as this was already an issue in our past in Atlantis. No matter how tempting, we should not allow any person or group to install microchips or AI technology on or in our human bodies. Our human body is extremely powerful, and the controlling powers will likely attempt to use these types of technology to suppress our awakening. No matter what promises are made, or conveniences may come from integrating the technology into our body, I suggest avoiding such hybridization and transhumanism while humanity still operates in 3D as hijacking is still possible and highly probable. The organic technology of our own human body is capable of telepathy, bilocation, astral travel, telekinesis, levitation, channeling higher consciousness beings, and so much more, and there is no need to give in to the allure of the promises made by Big Tech and other influential powers.

Healing

Energy medicine is the way of the future. One client described being in a safe haven community when global events were in chaos. She described a beam of light emanating from the center of the community that people who were awakening could see and travel towards to find the community. On the grounds of the community were many lightworkers with visible light emanating from their hands. She described Arcturian beings teaching advanced healing practices to humans and medical beds that rapidly heal people at the cellular level.

As the human consciousness opens, we will receive more information through channelings and hypnosis sessions like Illuminated Quantum Healing. We have tremendous amounts of information stored within our Akashic Records, our soul's memory bank. Illuminated Quantum Healing and the other quantum healing hypnosis modalities will be of great support during these next stages to help those who are ascending and to ease the suffering of those who are destined to exit the Earth realm.

Shifting to New Earth Relationships

Individuals are now finishing their karmic contracts in preparation for what is to come. Many people are finishing up karmic relationships and moving into supportive soul family relationships. Instead of the past's power and control techniques, these relationships are supportive, cooperative, and empower individuals to be their own Sovereign Self. Many are reporting that they have left the patterns of karmic romantic relationships of the past and are meeting their Divine Mirror or Twin Flame. More is spoken about twin flames, spiritual partnership, and sacred sexuality in the Sacral Chakra section.

What a relief to be in the presence of others who are genuinely loving and share the same energy signature. In these relationships, we can feel "HOME" through this highly resonant vibration. These beings are familiar to us, and we feel quickly in tune with one another with a depth that cannot be explained by how much physical interaction we have had in this life.

For some, this includes moving to a new home or geographic location, changing careers, or even being in a void space as it is not so clear what the next steps are. The void space is a natural part of this process. Rather than forcing action, it is best to meditate and reflect until you feel divinely guided and inspired to make a choice. Trust that you are being guided every step of the way.

We can look at spiritual relationships in four categories. I cannot remember the origin of the teaching, but I remember the four categories:

1. *Spiritual Teachers and Mentors.* These people embody and exemplify the consciousness and achievements that you aspire to.
2. *Spiritual Friends.* Those at a similar level of spiritual development. Your energetic frequency is similar, and you easily find resonance.
3. *Spiritual Acquaintances.* This type of friendship is where we often feel like mentors more than equals in terms of spiritual growth.
4. This last category is made of those people who are either unawakened and have little to no commonality with us or who could bring harm.

Many people get caught relating to level 3 and level 4 types and feel they are always helping others without reciprocation or feel that they are misunderstood and often get hurt. We should spend the majority of our time with the first two categories to fuel our expansion!

The Unveiling of Technologies and Knowledge

Throughout Earth's history, information has been suppressed and many powerful technologies have been hidden from humanity. This includes artifacts hidden by the Vatican, the Crown, shadow government projects, and secret subterranean programs. Some of this repressed information has been kept by service-to-self, and some has been "lost" until humanity was ready to remember the lost knowledge. In the coming years, these technologies and lost wisdom will return to humanity as we continue the transition to the New Earth reality.

Family of Light Reunion

Many countless spaceships and lightcraft are surrounding the planet at this time that are cloaked using advanced technology. More and more UFO sightings are happening all around the world. Many of these ships exist outside of the standard visible light spectrum. As we raise our vibration, more will begin to see them with their physical eyes or sense them with their inner eye.

Contact is beginning to increase around the planet between humanity and higher consciousness beings. Many people are experiencing apparitions of light beings or extraterrestrials. Many are experiencing them in their dreams or have begun channeling information from these other consciousnesses. The rekindling of relationships between humanity and the higher realms is beginning and will continue to increase. Soon, governments will start to disclose the truth of extraterrestrial visitation in preparation for the reunion of humanity with the Star Nations.

Soon, we will see lightships and spacecraft in our skies as the Star Nations and Hierarchy of Light return to the Earth to usher in the New Era. These beings will teach humanity advancements in Spirituality and Science and teach humanity how to be Cosmic Citizens as we collaborate and interact with many cosmic species and Beings of Light. Inner Earth life will go through a resurfacing process as the vibration rises. While some of these beings may have gotten used to Inner Earth, many are excited to stand with humanity in Unity and Love once more.

The New Earth will be a galactic meeting place for many races from the stars. Many advanced species will come here to share their knowledge and wisdom with humanity and one another. They will bring new plants, new animals, new songs, and new ideas. It will be a cosmic renaissance with everyone sharing from their hearts to uplift all of Life. With no more negative polarity upon the planet, everything will be done in service to the greater good and we will all sail beyond the horizons of everything we have ever conceived, known, or experienced.

While I am writing this book, the news stations have started disclosing more footage of UFOs. I wonder why they are showing this now? Is it truly to disclose what has been intentionally hidden from humanity, or is there a darker agenda behind it? The Controllers may push a false narrative of "threat" from ETs to use emotional manipulation to get humanity to give up more of its freedom. The nefarious ET presence has been here and has played a massive part in the control of humanity and the Earth. The Controllers will try all they can in these final stages to incite fear and separation. I have never heard of a threat of negative ET invasion; however, I have heard through documentaries of shadow project initiatives to stage an ET invasion, but I am assured that the craft we see in the skies are our allies and star family who are here to assist.

New Humanity

Fourth Density humanity of New Earth will not age in the way that we do now. Children will mature into adulthood but will not age beyond that until their soul has completed its mission and has aligned with an exit trajectory. There will be no illness, no suffering, and humanity will have complete freedom of life to create and play. If there are imbalances, clients describe healing beds that use crystalline technology, frequency, and sound to amplify wellness at the cellular/quantum level.

Earth will have fewer seasonal changes and less harshness in weather, and the whole of the planet will be in balance with incredible peace. Earth will return to the "vacation planet" status where no negativity exists, and peace and abundance are experienced by all. The emotional/mental body of humanity will be completely reset, and the lower astral planes will be cleared of distortion and negative entities. This will mean no more tormenting dreams, no more resentment, no more negative internal voices, and no hijacking of consciousness. People will understand one another and be connected through the heart and through telepathic communication with nothing to hide and plenty of love and connection to share. Not only will we share telepathy with one another but also through telepathic communication with Gaia herself and all of her kingdoms of Life. We will not possess the land because we clearly recognize Gaia as our Divine Sister and Earth Mother who provides us happily with all that we need. We will truly be a community of Light experiencing God's Kingdom upon the great cosmic garden of New Earth.

I have had a few powerful experiences where I was shown through vision and through my own body how the body and DNA will evolve into the new form.

I was taken into my body and DNA to show the gigantic mess that has become our DNA. Thousands upon thousands of years of ancestral trauma blocks our DNA. Even our unconscious and trauma-ridden words send entropic vibrations into our cells and tissues which lowers our vibrations in all our systems. Toxins from our food, water, and environment clog and distort the free flow of energy throughout our body. No one on the planet, at this time, has had a fresh start. We all are operating from significantly poisoned and damaged instruments on some level.

The new DNA is clean, clear, and perfectly reset to the Adamic DNA template. This gives the Light of our Divine Nature the freedom to broadcast through our DNA without being distorted or limited. This perfected DNA will open a wide array of abilities that are normal actions from our pure DNA but will seem miraculous from our current consciousness vantage point. We will be able to fly and bilocate to other points on Earth and beyond. Our new, bioluminous instrument will channel divine energy and intention to work harmonically with the consciousness of Gaia. We will be merged in unity consciousness and work symbiotically with all levels of life on the planet to maintain the harmony of our renewed paradise home. We will be able to work with the technology that is the consciousness of Nature and purify the waters, instantly raise forests up from the soil with our heartfelt intentions and psychic gifts. We will work harmoniously with one another as cooperative communities in celebration of Eternal Life and our reunion with our Family of Light.

In the times of Atlantis, we allowed Artificial Intelligence to be created outside of balance and Natural Law. Artificial Intelligence can be a dangerous creation, especially when being created by humans in the third dimension. We should avoid any type of inorganic alterations to our DNA and body before this shift. This includes microchips and inoculations that will be encouraged or even forced upon humanity by controlling forces. While I have heard of people in future timelines who were integrated with AI and microchips, it was way after we had shifted to the higher consciousness.

Housing on the New Earth

When clients visit future timelines of Earth, they describe a vibrant Earth with more color and light. They describe a beautiful aroma as all the waste and pollution has been removed with the support of the Hierarchy of Light. People commonly describe that many people will be living in tree house communities and dome structures. I assume that the energy is much better above ground, and one client shared that in Atlantis, she used a tree as a dimensional transport. Trees are a bridge, just like humans, to higher realms of existence. Some people describe domes and healing temples where sound healing and other spiritual training are conducted. These homes are intimately connected to Nature. One client described vines growing in her home, offering their fruits for her to eat. Another client said that if one were hungry, they could reach towards a tree branch as a flower transformed into an apple for them to eat. Another woman described going off into the forest to deliver a child alone. As she lay by a waterfall, plants, animals, and nature spirits came to her to assist her in pain-free birth.

Estimated Timelines for these Events

Please keep in mind that there is nothing to fear. All is in the hands of Source and Gaia as we make this transition. We are about to move into the big revelations of information which will cause a tremendous amount of emotional turmoil as people put the pieces together and understand what has been happening on the planet. I have heard that eventually a powerful energy wave will cause a split in dimensions, some ascending and the rest will play out the end of their contracts on 3D Earth as they have agreed to before incarnation. After the main event pulse, dramatic Earth changes will occur. After this stage the building up of new systems will take place as we establish harmony in the New Earth civilizations.

There are many timelines possible for this play-out. I am giving dates very loosely with zero attachment to those dates. I have heard through a few clients that much of this Grand Transformation of Life will occur by around 2027-2030 with at least two major energy events occurring before then, possibly one in 2022/2023 which will awaken many to their soul purpose. The Shadow Controllers will not be able to hold humanity down any longer as millions awaken simultaneously. We will be, and already are, an unstoppable Force of Light!

That means that we will be in a constant process of major multidimensional transformation over these next few years and mainstream society will be quite chaotic as all is revealed and transformed. We cannot even imagine the world we are about to manifest. Even as the world seemingly turns dark, I offer you these next transcriptions and visions of the future to help you stay focused on what is ours to inherit.

As we walk through the shadows of this collapsing reality, know in your heart of hearts that you are walking towards everything you have ever wanted and more. Keep your eye on the prize! I am assured over and over again that there is no turning back and that on all timelines Ascension happens. We will be victorious! Don't give up before the miracle!

Now we journey into the Akashic Database!

TWELVE

Manifestation of New Earth Prayer

As we close our journey through *The Illumination Codex* material, let us acknowledge, honor, and celebrate the myriad forms of our Oneself working towards higher harmony and consciousness unity across all times, dimensions, and realities. I wrote this prayer while visiting Glastonbury, UK. It is written in the pagan style and will have different elemental and directional associations if you are used to Native American prayer structure. This prayer is a powerful one to use when opening sacred space and is used now in this book to seal the benefits of reading this material and to open a portal for your next chapter of multidimensional expansion. Bless you all!

We call upon the energies of the East — the direction of the rising sun, birth and rebirth, and the element of air. We honor and evoke the wisdom of winged beings such as the birds, butterflies, and dragonflies who ride upon the air. We honor the cycles of breath, from the personal to the cosmic. We pray for the winds of the Earth to be cleansed and cleared for all generations to be able to enjoy the sweetness of breath. Let us embody the power of renewal and rejuvenation and be reminded of Life's and Spirit's eternal nature and the truth of our immortality.

We call upon the Light Beings and Spiritual Guardians of the East. Let us feel your presence NOW.

We call upon the energies of the South — the direction of the midday sun, the element of fire which burns, purifies, and transforms. We honor and evoke the wisdom of the sacred fire, the magma, and lightning. We call forth this energy to burn away that which does not serve the balance of Life. Purify our hearts and intentions and alchemize our essence so that we may embody our Divine Radiance.

We call upon the Light Beings and Spiritual Guardians of the South. Let us feel your presence NOW.

We call upon the energies of the West — the element of water and the direction of the setting sun. This is a place of endings that lead to new beginnings. A place of reflection and introspection. We honor and evoke the wisdom of the waterways, the lakes, rivers, and oceans, the cleansing rain, and the Living Waters within the Earth. We pray for our waters, both in and outside of our bodies, to be healed and purified in this eternal moment.

We call upon the Light Beings and Spiritual Guardians of the West. Let us feel your presence NOW.

We call upon the energies of the North and the element of Earth — the place of wisdom and rest, the place of our grandparents and ancestral lineages. We welcome the sacred energies and wisdom held within the bones of our ancestors. We honor and evoke the mountains' wisdom, mineral kingdoms, animal kingdoms, elemental kingdoms, crystalline kingdoms, and plant kingdoms. We ask for a special blessing for the healing and rejuvenation of the soil of the Earth. We honor our bodies, given to us by our Earth Mother, as temples for the indwelling of Eternal Spiritual Light.

We call upon the Light Beings and Spiritual Guardians of the North and our ancestors of Light and Wisdom. Let us feel your presence NOW.

We call upon the energies of above and the element of Ether. We invite into our awareness the loving presence of Mother/Father God, Source of our Being. We welcome the loving guidance of our Ascended Self, the Angelic Kingdom, Ascended Masters, Exalted Goddesses, the Elohim, and our star lineages.

We acknowledge the Source of Our Being and invite our Family of Light and our star lineages to be with us as we remember our divinity. Let us feel your presence NOW.

We call upon the energies of below and the love of Mother Gaia. We call forth remembering the wisdom of the Golden Ages of Gaia and the wisdom from our past lifetimes on the Earth. We honor and evoke the wisdom of the Inner Earth kingdoms and our Family within the Earth.

We call upon the Light Beings and Spiritual Guardians of the Below. Let us feel your presence NOW.

We call upon the energies of within, the gateway to the Kingdom of Heaven. We call forth and activate our sacred, crystalline heart and return to the truth of our Oneness, acknowledging the sacredness of all Life. We evoke and dream awake our Ascended Self. Whole. Radiant. And Free. Let us expand this prayer field into all dimensions, all timelines, all universes, and realities so that all of Creation may benefit from our Love.

May it be so! May it be now! And so, it is! OM.

ᴀSCENSION ʟEXICON

I have put together a list of words commonly used in this book and for the topics of awakening, spirituality, and ascension. These are not necessarily defined this way by others but are an excellent way to understand my writings in this book in a more clear and multidimensional way.

-A-

Adamic Form: Original perfected divine human form created for highly developed Light Beings to experience physical creation from within the physical dimension. Fourth Density (4D) body of the New Earth human connecting with oversoul consciousness, higher dimensional beings, and telepathic species.

Agartha: Ancient Inner Earth multi-species civilization with its own sun and ecosystem within the Earth. See *Inner Earth*.

Ain Soph: Kabbalistic term for Source before manifestation into form and translates to "Without Limit" as it is the unlimited creative potential behind all of Creation. Same as "Ineffable" in the Gnostic texts. Can also be written as "Ensof."

Akashic records: Higher-dimensional spiritual records of all experience past, present, and future. Each soul has one. So does each planet and so on.

alchemy: The application of spiritual knowledge to matter to create transformation. This is more commonly known with the Middle Ages' pursuits of turning simple metals into gold. High alchemy being the alchemy of soul/lightbody.

Ancient Egypt: Last golden age of Gaia when many beings held 4th, 5th, and 6th-dimensional consciousness before the descent into lower consciousness (forgetting).

Andromedans: Highly advanced star beings from the Andromeda galaxy assisting humanity's ascension.

Anunnaki: Star beings from the Nibiru system. Sumerian space "gods" who manipulated humanity for personal gain. Now most are in support of humanity's ascension.

apocalypse: 1. Greek word for "unveiling." 2. The dismantling of the mind control matrix and false projections from the controlling forces to reveal to humanity the ugly underbelly and karma of the collective consciousness upon the Earth from this creation cycle which is to be fully reconciled before the planet changes in dimension to Fourth Density New Earth. Not the "end" but a transitory phase into the next creation cycle.

Archons/Controllers: Term used to describe negatively polarized service-to-self, nonphysical, intelligent beings who siphon negative energy from humanity for their own gain using mind control tactics to keep humanity enslaved through fear and distorted consciousness. The controlling forces behind global institutions. Will be fully dismantled before the shift to New Earth.

Arcturians: Star beings from the constellation of Arcturus assisting Earth with Ascension.

Ascension/ascension: 1. The spiritual maturity process of a soul, moving from an unawakened state of mundane consciousness to multidimensional Source/God-realization described as the movement of the kundalini up the central channel, samadhi, moksha, nirvana, salvation... 2. The movement of Creation into greater states of Glory. 3. The current collective planetary transformation from 3D to 5D consciousness and the New Earth reality.

ascension symptoms: Physical, etheric, mental, and spiritual changes during ascension cycles. Includes headaches, emotional purging, detoxifications symptoms, multidimensional DNA reprogramming, body aches, vivid dreams, and beyond.

Ascended Master: Level of spiritual hierarchy of beings who have ascended in their consciousness enough to no longer need to incarnate in form for spiritual growth but may choose to incarnate to assist the ascension process of a species.

Atman: Divine origin identity, True Self, True Nature, the Witness Consciousness of a lifestream. Same as Brahman. Source Self. Eternally free.

aura: Electromagnetic field of subtle energy that surrounds and pervades the physical body. Contains ever-shifting patterns and geometries of light and vibration that create the template for the physical form.

-B-

biotransducer: organic instrument for transforming energy information for the purpose of manifestation and communication with the universal hologram and divine frequencies. Able to utilize advanced intelligence and spiritual information for the transformation of reality in the human environment.

bodhisattva: Sanskrit term for someone on the path of Buddhahood (ascension) who dedicates their path to the liberation of all beings from cycles of suffering. Able to achieve liberation but delays to assist others in consciousness expansion.

Brahman: The Absolute Reality. Source in impersonal, nonmanifest state. Pure Infinity Existence Consciousness Bliss, *Satchitananda.*

buddhi: the Intellect, reflected consciousness, enlightened consciousness in each person.

buddhic consciousness: enlightened consciousness expressed by *buddhi*, the vehicle for the soul, experienced as profound intuitive insight, unity, and bliss.

-C-

Cabal: Global elite network of negatively polarized service-to-self operatives and organizations working towards complete domination of humanity and planet Earth. See *Archons.*

causal consciousness: the higher mind capacity which utilizes soul memory and intuition to observe and understand manifestation multidimensionally.

centering: Alignment with one's divine nature and inner truth, activating a bridge between Gaia and the Divine through the heart center.

centropy: Regenerative electrification of matter-energy.

chakras: Spiraling transformers of subtle energy with seven primary vortices emanating from the central channel (*sushumna*) which govern our perception of the projected holographic reality and energize our mental and physical processes.

channeling: Opening one's consciousness and vessel as a conduit for subtle energy or other consciousnesses.

Christ: 1. Yeshua ben Joseph (Jesus) in his ascended Lightbody. Forerunner of christ consciousness as part of a divine plan for redemption and restoration of humanity and Earth back to a 4th Density collective. 3. A collective consciousness field that has many emanations and incarnated forms throughout the history of Creation. 4. Title given to one who has achieved consciousness mastery and is "anointed' by Light.

christ consciousness: Also called cosmic consciousness or 5D consciousness. Demonstrated by Jesus of Nazareth in his resurrected 4th Density body.

Christ/Magdalene Lineage: Genetic implantation of higher DNA coding through the offspring of Jesus and Mary. Descendants are worldwide and able to carry a higher light quotient and awaken more easily.

clairaudience: Clear hearing is the ability to hear messages from your Higher Self or spirit beings. This includes hearing the thoughts of other people.

clairgustance: Clear tasting is the ability to receive intuitive information through the sense of taste.

clairesalience: Clear smelling is the ability to intuit information through the sense of smell.

clairvoyance: Clear sight is the ability to perceive information through internal imagery.

clear channeling: Mediumship, or spirit channeling, is the ability to communicate with nonphysical beings and consciousness structures. This can include souls who have passed beyond the veil of physical life or beings that exist in other dimensions.

collective: Representing an entire group, i.e., human collective.

Collective Messiahship: The unification of ascending humanity with the intention of global restoration and ascendency.

cords: Subtle energy attachments that connect us to other beings. Can be negative if developed through limiting beliefs and distorted conditioning.

council: Group of beings joined together with a common focus (i.e., your spiritual council of guides who support your spiritual maturation across lifetimes).

Councils of Light: Groups of advanced spiritual beings that govern the evolution of consciousness and the biological forms of a certain experimental zone to encourage higher states of glory and harmony with the highest being the Universal Council of Light.

-D-

density: 1. Mass per volume. 2. Bandwidth of consciousness reality.

Descension/descension: To go down. The forgetting or falling asleep phases of consciousness. The stepping down of light frequency.

dharma: The noble path of awakening guided through alignment with the Divine through one's True Nature. Exemplified by the life path of beings like Jesus and the Buddha.

The Divine: The frequency emanation that governs and sustains all of Creation across many universes within universes. God Source and the Hosts of Heaven. See *Godhead*.

Divine Androgyny: Harmonic synergy between the divine masculine and divine feminine energetic expressions that results in perfect balance and cohesion.

Divine Creatorship: The birthright of a human to create their life with free-will choice in alignment with their Inner Source.

Divine Feminine: 1. Nurturing creative quality of the Divine 2. Archetypal, spiritual, and psychological ideal of the feminine energetic expression.

Divine Masculine: 1. Administrative quality of the Divine 2. Archetypal, spiritual, and psychological ideal of the masculine energetic expression.

DNA: Genetic blueprint for the development of an organism with both physical and subtle components. Ascended humanity will have 12 fully restored strands.

-E-

Earth Changes: Physical and subtle energetic changes that occur on the planet as it prepares to shift into the next creation cycle. Includes pole shifts, weather changes, seismic and volcanic activity, electromagnetic shifts, and more.

Elohim: First Creation. Creator beings with individual consciousness that work in groups to form Creation. Some created as service-to-all working in unity with Source. Some were created as service-to-self permitted to create in the illusion that they were separate from Source.

empath: Individual who is sensitive to the subtle energy such as thought, and emotional projections of others as they intuitively feel the mental/emotional body of others within their own mental/emotional realm. See *clairsentience*.

End Times: The closing of this current creation cycle where all karma must be balanced, and all shadow revealed so that Earth and spiritually activated humanity can begin the next creation cycle in 4th Density New Earth. See *apocalypse*.

energy: Subtle energy beyond the visible light spectrum ranging from pervasive to neutral to regenerative and life-enhancing. Everything is energy.

energy awareness: Perception of subtle energy in and around one's body.

energy matrix: Geometric organization of subtle frequencies that creates the base structure for the development of form.

entity attachment: Astral debris that has attached itself to a weakened energy system of a host as a source of sustenance and a way to live out "unfinished business." Quite common and easily resolved most of the time by a trained spirit releasement practitioner or energy medicine practitioner.

entropy: Decay and degeneration of matter-energy.

extraterrestrial: From outside of the Earth's biosphere including other planets and universes. There are countless species in our solar system, galaxy, super galaxy, and beyond. Infinite species in infinite realms of creation with many advanced civilizations with histories tracing back trillions of years.

evolution: See *Higher Evolution.*

-F-

false prophets: Teachers and prophets who use spiritual information for service-to-self agendas. Many religious leaders, spiritual teachers, and even those in the ascension community will have their true intentions revealed in the final phases of Ascension.

Family of Light: Physical and nonphysical beings who live their lives in alignment with the Oneness of Creation and the Divine Source. Includes the races of the Star Nations who hold 5D consciousness and higher and the Hierarchy of Light who tend to the many levels of Light Creation.

5D: Consciousness of humans living on the New Earth, can be referred to as christ consciousness or oversoul consciousness.

4D: Awakening stage of ascension bridging mundane consciousness with the New Earth consciousness.

frequency: 1. Rate of vibration measured in hertz (Hz). 2. Higher vibrational rate is likened to positivity and centropy and lower rate towards negativity and entropy.

-G-

Gaia: 1. Sentient Earth 2. Common name for the soul of Earth. Also called Terra.

Galactic Federation of Light: Intergalactic and ultraterrestrial collective of advanced beings who tend to the evolution of consciousness and biological forms throughout the Milky Way. Comprised of advanced scientists, engineers, medical personnel, and other areas of expertise needed to maintain order and balance in the galaxy.

genetic implantation: Seeding of new DNA into the gene pool to evolve a species into higher states of harmony or functionality. Used by the Star Nations and Hierarchy of Light to craft zones of biological experimentation.

gnosis: Direct experience of divine nature through one's own inner being and inner knowing that leads to higher understanding of the nature of the divine reality. See *Knowledge*.

Great Central Sun: Source of all levels of creation in this universe. Brings higher evolutionary coding from Divine Source into other central suns in the universal grid which flow to each solar system evolving each region in accordance with a Divine Plan for Higher Evolution. See *Ishawara*.

Great Divide: The bifurcation of consciousness amongst humanity during the end phases of the planetary ascension process. Includes physical movement across the Earth as humanity moves to be with others of shared consciousness and similar vibration and soul path. Two-world-spit of those who hold negatively polarized, service-to-self consciousness and those of positively polarized, service-to-all consciousness.

Great White Brotherhood: More accurately **Great White Siblinghood**. Ascended Masters, human and non-human, of all gender expressions organized into different orders or councils who tend to the evolution of consciousness and sometimes incarnate to bring new teachings and new energy. Many of these Ascended Masters have aspects of themselves on the planet now to assist the Ascension.

Greys: Extraterrestrial beings from Zeta Reticuli.

God: 1. Supreme Source of Creation 2. Divine Masculine, administrative quality of Godhead, Eternal Mind. See *Ishwara*.

Goddess: 1. Divine Feminine, nurturing, regenerative, creative aspect of the Godhead. 3. Mother God.

Godhead: The Divine Consciousness Source and its various emanations and functions.

Golden Ages: Times of high consciousness and harmony upon the Earth during the Precession of the Equinoxes. (e.g., Avalon, Lemuria)

grounding: The anchoring of one's physical and subtle bodies into the Earth's core through intention, diaphragmatic breathing, and visualization through the Root and Earth Star chakras.

guides: Spiritual beings who assist an incarnated being on their dharmic path towards liberation.

-H-

hara line: Central pillar of light connecting an individual with Gaia and Source.

heart-centered: Action born from inner truth and spiritual ethics through alignment with one's divine nature.

Hierarchy of Light: Various levels of divine consciousness forms, aspects of Source that serve different functions in the evolution of Creation. Ain Soph/Source, Elohim, Archangels, Angelic Realm, Ascended Masters, Ascended Goddesses, Interdimensional Beings, and Restored Humanity in Adamic Form. The Hosts of Heaven.

Higher Evolution: Beyond biological evolution and natural selection, the recoding of experimental zones of the hologram of Creation using divinely encoded frequencies projected through the stellar network which are coordinated by benevolent beings, physical and nonphysical, who serve the evolution of the Divine Plan throughout the Multiverse. Also includes introduction of new genetic expressions into the gene pool, new technologies, and new ideas to be used to evolve the creation into higher order.

Higher Self: 1. The mature part of our consciousness which operates in positively polarized, service-to-all consciousness and is connected to our divine nature. 2. Sovereign self. 3. Harmonic Divine/Human synthesis. 4. Oversoul. 5. Atman.

Holding space: A term used in spiritual growth and self-development circles that means "to hold suffering in an alchemical container of loving awareness so that it may heal."

Holy Spirit Shekinah: The feminine regenerative energy of the Divine. The "presence of God" in the physical dimension. Opening yourself to channel the divine presence begins an alchemical process of light activation that heals and restores all levels of one's being.

-I-

Inner Earth: Ancient and contemporary subterranean civilizations. Many beings went to Inner Earth before the destruction of Lemuria and

Atlantis. See *Agartha*.

intention: Inner resolve to direct one's focus and creative capacity towards a specific goal. *Sankalpa* in Sanskrit.

interdimensional: Existing between dimensions.

intuition: The ability to perceive energy information beyond the five senses before it has become physically manifested in reality. 2. Extrasensory perception.

involution: spiritual consciousness activation that begins as one moves through Ascension and sheds the mind's conditioning.

Ishwara: 1. personal expression of Source. 2. Source in purest manifested form. Commonly called "God" 3. Great Central Sun. 4. Universal Logos.

-J-

Jesus/Yeshua ben Joseph: Master of Light for Earth. Twin flame of Mary Magdalene. Supreme teacher of Divine Love and Ascension. Brought restored DNA and pure Christ Light to the Earth to activate the 4th Density Redemption Plan. Yeshua's cosmic oversoul legacy includes many star systems including the high spiritual schools of Light in the Pleiades and Sirius A and B. His arrival into this dimension of space was the Star of Bethlehem Lightship. His life path was supported by many galactic beings incarnated upon the Earth as well as many extraterrestrials and ultraterrestrial beings. 2. Incarnation of Ascended Master Lord Sananda.

-K-

karma: 1. The sum of a being's actions in this life and in previous existences, both positive and negative actions which influences the soul's path through incarnations.

Knowledge: "Gnosis," divine insight that activates higher consciousness and God-realization. Sanskrit *aparoksha*

kundalini: Serpentine energy originating at the base of the spine that ascends through the sushumna during the awakening process creating ecstatic spiritual expression.

-L-

Lemuria: First advanced human civilization. Often associated with the Pacific Ocean. Destroyed by major flooding and earth changes.

ley lines: Subtle energy pathways that carry evolutionary information across the planetary grid. Also called dragon lines, songlines, telluric lines.

Light: Regenerative divine energy emanations that exist beyond the typical visible light spectrum (Holy Spirit). Different than conventional light from lightbulbs.

Light beings: 1. General term for nonphysical beings of divine origin. See *Family of Light.*

lightbody: 1. subtle body 2. Vital, lower, and higher mind sheaths. 3. Transmigrating soul

Light Conception: The act of conceiving a child directly from the spiritual realms without the need of sperm from a physical being.

Light language: 1. Language spoken through connection to the Divine Presence. Activates multidimensional healing and powerful internal experiences with healing frequencies. Gift of the Holy Spirit, the regenerative creative frequency that quickens and restores all levels of Life. Can be self-initiated or pushed through from the Higher Self and the Divine.

Light Seed: Higher-dimensional, light-encoded genetic material used for Light Conception and altering the genetic composition of a species. Aka *Immaculate Conception.*

Lightship/lightship: Divine craft made by one individual's lightbody/merkaba or a merged merkaba from more than one being for the purpose of interdimensional travel through space-time, stargates, and higher light realms.

Love: Beyond egoic love, unconditional love that is naturally expressed when one develops love for the divine and a service-to-all intention. *Agape* love.

lokas: Sanskrit word for the planes of existence.

loosh: energy of suffering and death harvested by negative human, extraterrestrial, and interdimensional beings which is used to fuel nefarious agendas.

Lyrans: Star beings from the constellation of Lyra. Most commonly known race is the feline beings. First humanoid race in the Milky Way. Original 144,000 oversoul starseeds to bring the human species to Earth.

-M-

magic(k): Use of universal, natural law, and intention to manifest. Can be either service-to-self (dark) or service-to-all (light).

manifestation: The materialization of intention into form.

mantra: Holy names and phrases repeatedly spoken or thought which generate divine thoughtforms to reprogram the physical, etheric, and mental bodies opening one's consciousness to higher perception, divine insight, and union with the Divine. Use of mantra repatterns the DNA, clearing distortion and debris and reprogramming it into higher order and functionality for the projection of divine consciousness light.

Mary Magdalene: Twin Flame and Divine Partner of Jesus. Ancient Egyptian Priestess. High initiate from the Pleiades, Venus, and other high consciousness realms. Arrived at Earth with Yeshua in the Star of Bethlehem Lightship. Gave birth to the offspring of Jesus. This lineage is spread throughout the world.

maya: Illusion. Projecting and veiling power of Source. All that has form and name which tests our ability to see the all-pervasive divine consciousness that supports all manifestations.

meditation: Conscious focusing of the mind on a single object.

merkaba: Divine light vehicle in the auric field that gives one the ability to travel to the higher light realms. Introduced back to humanity through Elijah.

Michael: Archangel who protects and defends all levels of Creation and biological life.

mindfulness: The practice of bringing our life's gross and subtle manifestations into the light of our awareness to observe life in nonduality. Nondual awareness is the ability to see beyond the illusion of duality and see with the eyes of loving awareness.

Mother Mary: Cosmic divine being, a Master soul, who incarnated to give birth to Jesus. High priestess of Ancient Egypt and master teacher of the cosmic priestess arts.

multidimensional: Existing in multiple planes of consciousness, i.e., physical, etheric, mental, and various spiritual dimensions.

Multiverse/multiverse: Universes within universes creating the totality of Creation. What Jesus spoke of when he referred to his "Father's house with many mansions."

-N-

nadis: Pathways of subtle energy in the body. There are said to be 72,0000 that weave in and around the physical body.

New Earth: 1. Higher density light spectrum reality of the ascended Earth. 2. Kingdom of Heaven on Earth.

nirvanic consciousness: liberated consciousness which has transcended suffering, limited egoic identity, and karmic cycles.

-O-

Orion: Constellation with ancient intelligent races with varying levels of consciousness and ranges of polarity. Factions of Reptilian and humanoid beings from Orion fought against Lyrans in the long galactic war.

oversoul: Higher consciousness identity of a soul. Where your individual soul comes from. Collective consciousness of myriad life streams and incarnations. 4th Density/5D Self.

-P-

past life regression: Form of hypnosis or shamanic journeying that evokes information from a client's subconscious mind from previous lifetimes.

Pleiadians: Star beings from the constellation of Pleiades, a highly advanced light consciousness school in our great universe. Cousins of humanity. They implanted upgraded DNA in humanity to open our spiritual connection.

prayer: Approach to the Divine through thought or word which opens the pathways for the living Light to infuse the one who is praying with love and divine insight.

priest: Male devotee of the Divine in service to the illumination of collective consciousness and the ascension of humanity. Administers the will and knowledge of the divine upon the Earth as well as the regenerative, healing presence of the divine feminine.

priestess: Female devotee of the Divine. Often connected to the Goddess. Embodies the wisdom of the divine feminine mothering principle of the Godhead. Matures consciousness in the community into higher states of creativity, sensuality, and grace.

psychic: One who has extrasensory perception. See *intuition*.

pyramids: Sacred architectural sites around the Earth built by various extraterrestrial and ultraterrestrial beings connecting the pathways of vital energy of the Earth with the universal energy grid for the reprogramming of life upon planet Earth. Act as broadcast and receiving systems for information used for planetary evolution.

Prakriti: Manifested reality, transactional reality as opposed to Absolute Reality, maya.

Purusha: Indwelling witness of Creation, Absolute Reality, Brahman, Pure Consciousness. Source Consciousness.

-Q-

quantum: Dealing with the holographic reality and fabric of Consciousness and creation.

quantum consciousness: Holographic consciousness connecting to the matrix of Creation with the ability to focus across time and space through nonlocality and consciousness projection.

quantum healing: Rapid, multidimensional healing that works at the cellular and subtle levels to bring the body's systems into homeostasis. Can be done through psychic processes, shamanic and energy medicine practices, hypnosis, quantum healing technology, star technology, and divine emanations. This is the medicine of New Earth.

quantum mysticism: Emerging evolutionary synthesis between science, metaphysics, and spirituality used to understand Consciousness and the laws that govern Creation.

Qumran: Ancient, multigenerational esoteric Essene community by the Dead Sea in present-day Israel that lived in complete recognition of the Divine through the study and embodiment of divine mystery teachings. Secretive community with advanced star knowledge and superhuman spiritual abilities. Traded knowledge with other global mystery schools and was home and school to Yeshua, Jesus of Nazareth. Yeshua's children studied here as well.

-R-

Reiki: 1. Japanese word meaning spiritual intelligence life force. 2. Intelligently-encoded, divine, redemptive, and regenerative energy from Source. 3. A gift of the Holy Spirit.

Redemption Plan: Cosmic and galactic initiative to restore humanity and Earth back to 4th Density as in the times of Lemuria. Includes genetic implantation, restoration of planetary grid, and operatives incarnating as human to bring new ideas and technologies, broadcasting intelligent and spiritual coding into the biofield of Earth and humanity, and more.

Reptilians: Reptilian humanoid star beings who have had a "negative" influence on Earth who have mostly evolved to positive polarity. Humans have reptilian DNA that gives us our ego mind to assist our perseverance in evolving.

reincarnation: The act of being born again into a new lifestream for the purpose of spiritual growth.

resonance: In spiritual terms, harmonic, synchronous vibrations between two or more objects.

Raphael: Archangel who administers to healing.

-S-

sacred sexuality: Alchemical sexual expression with the intention of uniting with the divine through one's own erotic spiritual nature. Can be practiced alone or with a partner(s).

sacred sites: Holy power spots spread across the planet that form a web of vortex points for subtle energy pathways of the Earth.

samsara: 1. Wheel of Karma 2. rounds and rounds of incarnations on the path of Ascension 3. Suffering mind. 4. Cycles of suffering.

samskaras: Grooves in the mind that create reactive emotions forming our biases, habits, and tendencies. Can be seen as negative or positive.

Self: Divine Self as opposed to the egoic self which is trapped in worldly conditioning.

sentience: The ability to feel, be conscious, or have one's own subjective experience.

service-to-all: Positively polarized, dedicated intention, thought, and action towards the Greater Good and Higher Love as an extension of one's True Self.

service-to-self: Negatively polarized, gives power to false self, ego. Can seem "positive" as intentions can be different than presentation.

sin: Intention, thought, and action that goes against one's inner light that causes an immediate depletion of life force and positive vibration. Serves the egoic self. There is no judgment for this from higher realms. All is for learning and growth. 2. Fear-based judgment system created by religion which connects to belief systems that limit the indwelling of spiritual light by creating perpetual states of fear, shame, and guilt. 3. The fundamental illusion of separation from Source.

Sirians: Star beings from the region of the Sirius A and Sirius B binary star system who have a long, positive history with humanity and are assisting Earth now.

Solaris: Central sun and stargate of our solar system which emanates supraliminal coding for the evolution of the myriad lifeforms in our solar system.

soul: 1. Subtle bodies which transmigrate from one life to the next. See *lightbody.*

spiritual partnership: A relationship that is supported by the desire to assist one another in awakening and healing.

soul contracts: Pre-designed plan and agreements before incarnating for the balancing of karma to propel the path of liberation and ascension. Includes soul agreements between individual souls to play out certain catalyst roles.

soul purpose: Divine intention for a soul for its incarnation encompassing the themes to be explored and lessons to be learned throughout a lifestream. Generally, a soul's purpose is to awaken to Higher Love and Divine Truth.

sovereign: natural consciousness state of the Atman/Self/Inner Source. Human beings embody and reclaim sovereignty through involution and higher consciousness evolution. Able to have agency in all areas of life. Self-regulated. Self-governed.

stargate: Portal used for transportation between long distances and different dimensions.

Star Nations: Space-traveling intelligent species, some positive, some negative, some neutral in relation to humanity and the Earth.

starseeds: Visitors from other schools in the multiverse who have volunteered to live a human life to assist the Ascension of Gaia and humanity. Many of which have experienced ascension mastery in other lifetimes. The best ascension masters from the universe are here on the planet or around the planet in crafts at this time.

substratum: 1. Foundational, base material 2. Source/Brahman/Atman/Pure Consciousness.

superluminal: 1. faster than light

synchronicity: The meeting of two or more seemingly unrelated events or objects that come together in a meaningful way that could even be perceived as divinely coordinated.

-T-

timelines: Pathways of probable events. Infinite potentials and realities fractal out and converge at particular junction points in "time" where choice points exist for the next fractal offshoots of timeline potentials. We are currently moving with multiple timeline potentials for Ascension events that lead to one inevitable event, 4th/5th Density New Earth. Timelines are constantly in flux depending on personal moment-to-moment choices from individuals or the collective meaning the future is never "fixed" but is always in flux. This is the reason why some psychics see different potential probabilities playing out in the future.

3D: Standard human consciousness in its unawakened state, fear/duality-based consciousness which is heavily programmed and hypnotized by the false matrix, the conditioning of the world, and the mind control techniques from the Archons.

Elders: Highest divine council. Progenitors of all cultures in the multiverse.

Twin Flames: Emanations of the same oversoul who assist one another in Ascension. Often uniting at the end of karmic cycles to serve Consciousness. Most commonly thought of as two people in Divine Partnership, but there can be more.

-U-V-W-Y-

Unified Field: The hologram of Creation, the Quantum Field, where all energies and manifestations arise from connecting all through Source Consciousness.

ultraterrestrial: Beings from beyond the physical plane, higher density beings in higher density forms.

vibration: The invisible, subtle layers of matter that form the basic templates for physical reality through repetitive oscillation.

Wisdom: Insight into the Divine Mysteries of Creation and the Godhead that connects us with higher states of divine love and divine grace. See *Knowledge, gnosis.*

walk-in: Exchange of souls during an incarnation. Typically occurs when the original soul consciousness assigned to the body can no longer continue an incarnation from trauma or some other way of vital depletion. A fresh soul consciousness is brought in to accomplish a certain task. Frequently used to bring highly developed galactic beings into the Earth for mission-oriented tasks.

Yeshua ben Joseph: See *Jesus* and *Christ*.

Recommended Reading

The Three Waves of Volunteers and The New Earth by Dolores Cannon
They Walked with Jesus by Dolores Cannon
Jesus and the Essenes by Dolores Cannon
Between Death and Life by Dolores Cannon
Keepers of The Garden by Dolores Cannon
Five Lives Remembered by Dolores Cannon
Return of the Bird Tribes by Ken Carey
Anna: Grandmother of Jesus by Claire Heartsong
Light on Life by B.K.S. Iyengar
The Yoga Sutras of Patanjali (many translations available)
Living Buddha, Living Christ by Thich Nhat Hahn
Reconciliation: Healing the Inner Child by Thich Nhat Hahn
Peace is Every Step by Thich Nhat Hahn
The Path of Energy by Dr. Synthia Andrews
The Seat of the Soul by Gary Zukav
The Book of Knowing and Worth by Paul Selig
The Diamond in Your Pocket by Gangaji
The Magdalen Manuscript: The Alchemies of Horus & the Sex Magic of Isis by Tom Kenyon and Judi Sion
The Kybalion by Three Initiates
Aparokshanubhuti by Adi Shankara
The Upanishads
The Bhagavad Gita
Drig Drishya Viveka
The Keys of Enoch by J.J. Hurtak
Pistis Sophia translated by J.J. Hurtak
The Secret Doctrine by H.P. Blavatsky
Etheric Double by A.E. Powell
The Causal Body and the Ego by A.E. Powell
Regression: Past-life Therapy for Here and Now by Samuel Sagan
Entity Possession: Freeing the Energy Body of Negative Influences by Samuel Sagan

The Illumination Codex

THE ILLUMINATION CODEX
GATEWAY ONE

Ascension Initiation

Keys for Higher Evolution

Michael Garber

THE ILLUMINATION CODEX
GATEWAY TWO PART ONE

Quantum Origins

Keys for Ancient Cosmology

Michael Garber

THE ILLUMINATION CODEX
GATEWAY TWO PART TWO

Cosmic Christ Transmissions

The Ministry of Light

Michael Garber

THE ILLUMINATION CODEX
GATEWAY FOUR

Chakra Yoga Discourse

Keys for Higher Consciousness

Michael Garber

THE ILLUMINATION CODEX
GATEWAY TWO PART THREE

New Earth Transmissions

Future Timelines of Gaia

Michael Garber

THE ILLUMINATION CODEX
GATEWAY THREE

Path of Awakening

Keys for Transfiguration

Michael Garber

THE ILLUMINATION CODEX
GATEWAY FIVE

Laying of Hands
Reiki & Beyond

Michael Garber

WWW.NEWEARTHASCENDING.ORG

Support Our Initiatives

Ron and I have dedicated our lives to supporting this Grand Transition. We stand alongside all of you as humanity awakens to its True Nature and becomes a People of Light in the heavenly reality of New Earth.

New Earth Ascending is dedicated to assisting people to realize their divinity and manifest that truth in every aspect of their life. For more information about New Earth Ascending or to contact Michael, please scan the QR code below for a list of resources and links, or visit *www.newearthascending.org*. Be sure to check out our courses including the Illuminated Quantum Healing practitioner course.

New Earth Ascending is a registered 508 (c)(1)(a) Self-Supported Non-profit Church Ministry with a global outreach. We greatly appreciate your support as we create new systems, communities, and schools for the development of the New Earth civilization. If you would like to make a tax-deductible donation to support our mission, please go to:

https://donorbox.org/donationtonewearthascending

Scan with a smart device camera for more information including websites, social media, and more! Bless us all!

www.ingramcontent.com/pod-product-compliance
Lightning Source LLC
Chambersburg PA
CBHW071359120626
46546CB00002B/756